# The
# Madwoman
## and the
# Roomba

ALSO BY SANDRA TSING LOH

*The Madwoman in the Volvo*

*Mother on Fire*

*A Year in Van Nuys*

*Aliens in America*

*If You Lived Here, You'd Be Home by Now*

*Depth Takes a Holiday*

# The
# Madwoman
## and the
# Roomba

MY YEAR OF DOMESTIC MAYHEM

Sandra Tsing Loh

**W. W. NORTON & COMPANY**
*Independent Publishers Since 1923*

Names and other potentially identifying characteristics of people and places mentioned in this book have been changed.

Copyright © 2020 by Sandra Tsing Loh

The lyrics/words to "Mr. Loh" by Boy Hits Car are taken from the book *Brief Accounts of Consciousness* by Cregg Rondell.

For information about permission to reproduce selections from this book, write to Permissions, W. W. Norton & Company, Inc., 500 Fifth Avenue, New York, NY 10110

For information about special discounts for bulk purchases, please contact W. W. Norton Special Sales at specialsales@wwnorton.com or 800-233-4830

Manufacturing by Sheridan    .
Book design by Ellen Cipriano
Production manager: Lauren Abbate

Library of Congress Cataloging-in-Publication Data

Names: Loh, Sandra Tsing, author.
Title: The madwoman and the Roomba : my year of domestic mayhem / Sandra Tsing Loh.
Description: First edition. | New York, N.Y. : W. W. Norton & Company, [2020]
Identifiers: LCCN 2019052108 | ISBN 9780393249200 (hardcover) | ISBN 9780393249217 (epub)
Subjects: LCSH: Loh, Sandra Tsing. | Women authors, American—Biography. | Middle-aged women—Biography.
Classification: LCC PS3562.O459 Z46 2020 | DDC 818/.5403 [B]—dc23
LC record available at https://lccn.loc.gov/2019052108

W. W. Norton & Company, Inc., 500 Fifth Avenue, New York, N.Y. 10110
www.wwnorton.com

W. W. Norton & Company Ltd., 15 Carlisle Street, London W1D 3BS

1  2  3  4  5  6  7  8  9  0

# Contents

# Contents

# Preface

Ah, FIFTY-FIVE. The golden years! The heady career summiting, ripening emotional maturity, the confident, gazelle-like loping with a surfboard toward the Pacific blue waters of a sagely planned retirement.

That's what we find in airline magazines, anyway. (Which I read deep in coach, starving because I haven't sagely planned anything, not even a snack that costs less than an eighteen-dollar Wolfgang Puck quinoa/aioli wrap.) Nowadays, coast to coast, I discover, it seems fit "silver foxes" are busy not just surfing but using their American Express Platinum cards to start their own rockin' garage bands, hitting a rad chord and doubling over in laughter as their bangs (really, they have bangs?) fly forward.

But no! My fifty-fifth year was more like living a disorganized twenty-five-year-old's life in a malfunctioning eighty-five-year-old's body. (And I don't mean Ruth Bader Ginsburg's—she is a superwoman who, if arm-wrestled, would clearly dislocate my shoulder.) It felt like trying to live Arianna Huffington's thrilling global values without her staff (or dry cleaner). It was like junior high without the carbs.

Let's talk, for a moment, about "retirement"—a word I've never been able to hear without dropping into a kind of Zen waking sleep state. (And now "IRA!" is the sound of bankers laughing.) Let's look at what many baby boomers are doing in this "Second Act of Life." (Yes, that's what my seventy-two-year-old retired Gestalt therapist friend calls it, without irony. Of course, she also wears Tibetan and Native American jewelry without irony—she is from Pennsylvania—but I digress.)

Here's what the boomers are doing—compared to activities in my own household:

*Boomers: Oh! We just spent four rhapsodic weeks this summer learning to make bread from Master Chef Ennio from the Food Channel in a sumptuous Tuscan farm villa.*

Sandra: On a recent cobbled-together trip to New York, our Airbnb "bachelor pad" (the only listing without prohibitive cleaning fees) had a single nightstand (next to the futon) bearing action figures, hand lotion, and a box of Kleenex. You do the math.

*Boomers: We are building a second home on land we bought ten years ago on a verdant remote island off the coast of Seattle.*

Sandra: The closest I'll get to the invigorating scent of the ocean is half-off oysters via Groupon Happy Hour. But those gastrobar Happy Hour menus are so confusing ("It's $3 off on 'well' drinks *before* five? What *is* a sunchoke?"). Eighty dollars later you're still starving. It's a recurring bagatelle (fancy words at least are free) we call "highway gastrobbery."

*Boomers: Steven has been learning to speak Khmer in preparation for our six-week Norwegian Silver Star Cruise to Cambodia.*

Sandra: I have to admit, I am obsessed with those glossy cruise pamphlets that fall like satiny papaya skins out of the Sunday *New York Times* (which our household purchases at the reduced "teacher's rate" of forty-nine dollars/month). Not only can we not afford $15,000 per person, I couldn't even afford the tasteful luxury/casual musliny blouses and fine linen palazzo pants all the serenely medicated salt-and-pepper-haired cruisers seem to be wearing. (In neutral colors! What about red wine stains? Once again—"middle" age— the dry cleaning alone!)

The only aquatic vacation my partner Charlie (he of the 2000 VW Beetle that smells like melted crayons) and I could afford was a three-day Carnival Cruise to Mexico. A traumatic Mr. Toad's Wild Ride (it's in the chapter entitled "101 Arguments Against 'Summer Fun'"), this floating DMV from hell was survivable only via the weed Charlie's mobile L.A. delivery service had prescribed for his (put Modelo beer can down to make big air quotes) "glaucoma."

Which is to say, technically, yes, I *am* a baby boomer (those born between 1946 and 1964), but my birth year—1962—was at the drooping tail of the boom. Born late in the game, think less true boomers than "Baby boom tastes on a Gen X budget," or "X-booms." (This can also sometimes look like "First World guilt on a Third World budget," resulting in what I call "Second World problems," but more on that to follow.) Now in "middle age" (for those planning to live to 120), the boomers are those silver-haired surfers (former doctors and attorneys) loping toward several million in retirement. By contrast, the "life hack" many of us aging X-booms have worked out regarding our retirement, health care, and leisure activities? Two words: "medical cannabis." (PS: The people who buy that "six-dollar red table wine blend" whose black-and-red label features a devil with horns or a woodcut of a pirate with some sort of medieval or Old English font on it, because as you know, an ornate font with lots of serifs suggests . . . classier . . . wine? Us!)

Okay, let me double back to say the cannabis thing may be overstated. I myself have always had little tolerance for pot. In "midlife," Charlie has tried to give me just enough "glaucoma medication" so I can tolerate *Game of Thrones*, but the result is always me losing consciousness fifteen minutes in and yet still waking up the next morning covered with a dragon breath's worth of Maple Bacon Kettle Chips crumbs. This is an amazing new menopausal innovation: sleep-eating.

However, it's no secret that our "whirling blue marble" has been going through some tumultuous, almost apocalyptic-feeling times lately, about which literally millions of words have been written. (Bumper sticker: WHERE ARE WE GOING, AND WHY ARE WE IN THIS HANDBASKET?) So even if one isn't getting stoned regularly, though no judgments if you are, I do think, as we struggle through day by day, there's something to be said for checking out a little occasionally, taking a breath, and finding some restorative joy—or at least some humor, dammit—in the small things.

So this, in short, is what this book is: a simple year in midlife. True, being this age did not seem golden, but feeling old and young at the same time can turn out to have silver linings. ("Gratitude" is not just a word on a throw pillow any more, although it is, in fact, also a word on a throw pillow.) Yes, the daily news is surreal—but the Walmart reading glasses I bought for the fun Tina Fey frames with the slightly too-low prescription—fuzzes it. Yes, there are some weird hip-joint things going on, but no more periods—f@#$ing awesome! Yes, the personal trainer you booked is commanding you to do burpies, but that's the beauty of not being in junior high any more—fire him!

Speaking of junior high, this year my golden years included parenting my somewhat maturing/somewhat not school-age daughters. This is the year I woke up from all of that you-go-girl nurturing ("And do we feel you have a soy allergy, honey?") to full-on freaking out about college. There were some unexpected (and I blush to say, not entirely unwelcome) funerals. There were the joys and surprising annoyances of spending the "Second Act" of one's life with one's "soulmate." (We are both "bohemian"; we are both messy; we both do not understand home repair—or pest control. Charming at twenty—not so charming approaching sixty! Although, as always, those Tina Fey/slightly-too-low-a-prescription reading glasses help take the edge off.)

And in fact . . . are we so different?

I sense you too need a break.

Take a load off.

Pull up a virtual ($1,000-off!) Costco massage chair. Let it pound your buttocks while a Roomba (guilt-free housekeeping) gently circles.

I'll put Pandora on to some soothing spa music, never mind that it is neither spa nor music. Let me pour you a glass of "varietal" wine with a fourteenth-century wizard on the label (don't worry—it has been "decanting" since Tuesday).

Forget the bigger world; let's celebrate the smaller world. Relax. Enjoy. Have a laugh.

When the world has gone mad, it's mad not to!

# The
# Madwoman
## and the
# Roomba

# The Tooth

I T's THAT MOMENT that comes only in dreams.

I'm standing in my kitchen in the gauzy soft-focus pocket of the midafternoon. 3:15. The quiet space between lunch and cocktail hour.

I've just gotten off a family conference call with my older sister Kaitlin, known within the family hierarchy as Eldest Daughter, Alpha Dog, or, to the younger ones, Tiger Aunt K. The territory under her vast military command is that of estates, trusts, elder care, life insurance, property deeds, and safety deposit boxes with possible forgotten silk kerchiefs of family gems.

Sam was also on the call. Affable, seventeen years old, the first Loh grandchild (of five), Sam is applying to college. According to Sam's perhaps admirably Zen dad (my brother Eugene, an engineer), Sam's GPA is "somewhere in the high 3's if you count AP classes." Sam's SAT's? Oblique, slightly tortuously phrased answer: "There are kids who have been known to have gotten into college with SAT scores somewhere in that range."

Tiger Aunt K has gone around the back, done some digging of her own, reporting that Sam has a 3.987 GPA—basically a 4.0, right?—and a surreally high SAT score that sounds like my weight on Jupiter, but which according to the "new" scoring is apparently well up into the 90s percentage-wise. These stats more than match those of his late mother, who went to Stanford, his first choice, right before UCLA, UC Berkeley, and, for safety, UC San Diego.

The one problem?

The personal essay. Here Sam needed his two aunts' help. As they say, It Takes a Village. Tiger Aunt K directs a K–12 STEM nonprofit, so is no stranger to energetic grant writing. I am a freelance writer, theater artist, adjunct teacher of science communication . . . I am no stranger to putting a "sounds more professional than it really is" face on things.

He read us the prompt: " 'Tell us about a personal quality, talent, accomplishment, contribution or experience that is important to you. What about this quality or accomplishment makes you proud and how does it relate to the person you are?' "

There was a beat.

Sam followed it with a sound like "Henh?"

Tiger Aunt K pounced in, eager, Tony Robbins-like: "What are your *passions*, Sam? That's all they're asking. What do you *love to do?*"

"Well, you know, just stuff." His inflections now went up, as though tentatively fishing. "Biking . . . ? Running . . . ? Hanging out with my friends . . . ?"

"But what *drives* you?" she pushed on, inspirationally. "Aren't you driven to learning, doing, inventing, creating? Think back to your childhood!"

I remembered that when Sam was six, when playing chess, he liked to attack with his king. Those pawns would fan out and, instead of castle-ing, his king would come out kicking, one square at a time. Not a killer strategy, but highly original.

"Legos," Sam said. "I've always built stuff with Legos . . ."

"Good," I said, encouragingly. "That suggests a native love of building . . ."

"Which clearly suggests," Tiger Aunt K quickly added, whipping up a heady self-actualization soufflé, "that Sam has a passion for international travel so he can visit African villages that need him to build water towers that are probably solar powered!"

"Yes!" I agreed. Sam's light protests were drowned out by my sister and I congratulating each other. No matter, her angle was brilliant—he would come round.

I now gaze dreamily out the kitchen window into the backyard. Tree branches sway in the sun. There's a graceful flutter of leaves. The world hovers before me, I hover outside of it. On the counter the NYT Tuesday crossword sits, not too hard, the perfect one, a quick little reward. I'm enjoying the coolness of the refrigerator, open before me. I find this a most relaxing way to snack, standing, no utensils, just hand to mouth, before a world of possibility. An open refrigerator door is a personal midafternoon wormhole to crawl into, a cosmic way station, a psychic rest stop.

It isn't really eating. It's just pausing before a crumpled paper bag of last night's Zankou chicken. Hello, friend! I pull off a morsel, take a hearty bite. It's so moist and tender. Though it seems to contain a small round pebble.

Hm. I pull it out—sometimes with Zankou, L.A.'s gourmet Armenian chicken chain, they're in such a hurry to stuff those blue-and-red take-out bags, a pepper may accidentally fall into your hummus— Though this is more like a popcorn kernel, or little piece of bone—

I fumble around in the reading glasses bowl, a lopsided blue ceramic one of my daughters made years ago at Gifted Children's Camp— Inside is a snarl of reading glasses, half missing a stem—

Glasses on, I look at the pebble. In contour, color, and sedimentary detail, it harkens back to a more prehistoric time. Burnt sienna, ancient, and mottled, it's like a small chunk from some caveman tool or terra-cotta pot, from some long-forgotten Assyrian dig.

With dawning horror I take an experimental fingertip up into the left back corner of my upper palate. It's the location of a weirdly sharp-edged molar that I would call just a bit "squeaky." The tooth has long had a filling, I think, from early adulthood, that has perhaps understandably gotten a bit loosened—

But no. This is no filling.

I am holding a piece of tooth. In my hand.

I feel my knees buckle. I collapse against the kitchen counter.

Obviously, by age fifty-five, I've lived through more than a few traumatic life events: illness, death, birth. (Never mind how I often wished for a martini-strength epidural drip that would begin in the second trimester and last until my kids turned twenty-one.) I've lived those totemic bleak life moments—pushing open those double doors to the ICU, or to the horrible new assisted living facility with your panicked aging parent. But with the big stuff, at least, you typically have a moment to pop three Advils, to arrange your face, to arm yourself with a stiff bouquet of flowers from the fluorescent-lit gift shop.

The last time my knees literally buckled was some ten years ago when, after a shower, I saw my towel seeming to breathe with small dark flecks. I shrieked, sprinted to the back porch, locked the door behind me, and called 911. "It's an invasion," I told the female dispatcher. "Should we call the CDC?"

"You have lice," she said. "Go buy some RID."

But those were temporary visitors. This chunk *has come out of my mouth.*

I call Charlie.

"Hello?" he says. Then: "Yes, the registration—"

Charlie is at AAA trying to do a "work-around" for the fact that his 2000 VW Beetle rarely passes a smog check. "The car runs fine, it just makes smog!" he keeps repeating to anyone who will listen, as though smog testing is a violation of the bug's basic right to exist.

"Argh . . ." I moan. "My tooth . . . fell out!"

"No it didn't," my WASP partner says immediately. When it comes to bad news, sunny denial is Charlie's reflex response.

"I'm looking at it. In my hand. Glasses on."

He has to drop the pretense.

"Does it hurt?" he asks.

"No, it doesn't."

"That's good."

"Is it?" I find my mood brightening. I flash on a freeway billboard I've seen a lot of a smiling brunette, eyes dreamily closed, under the magical caption: SLEEP THRU DENTISTRY.

A somewhat circular discussion ensues. It is true that I've stopped going to my dentist in Van Nuys since my move to Pasadena— More than, was it four, five, six years ago—? Oh God.

"You can see *my* dentist," Charlie offers. "Dr. Melvoin."

"Jack Black's dentist?" I ask. Charlie is always one step away from stardom, as he's a freelance theater producer. (True, there isn't much theater in L.A., but fortunately, nor are there many theater producers.) His son's pediatrician had the dubious honor of being the father of Hollywood madam Heidi Fleiss. I myself had my veneers done by yet another "dentist to the stars"—unfortunately, the "star" was one of those affable old character actors fourth barstool from the left on *Cheers* rather than a real star with a real nervous condition like Barbra Streisand.

"But wait," I say, "wasn't Dr. Melvoin arrested for that thing?"

"Oh yeah," Charlie says.

"When did you last see him?" I say accusingly.

"I think I was still living back in Eagle Rock?"

Somehow this gives me an opportunity to lash out at my partner. "Good lord! Look at us! We're just show trash, aging bohemians who keep trying to phone this all in! We're in our fifties now—the artsy 'college' thing isn't going to hack it. We can't just throw a paisley shawl over a peed-on futon anymore! We're falling apart!" I fling one final triumphant—if slightly tortuously phrased—salvo at him: "There's probably something about retirement we should be doing also!"

UPON HANGING UP, I realize this is an emergency situation. There's no longer any pretending.

I now remember how my web designer friend Katie Lazar always said how she had the best, most gentle dentist. Trouble is, Katie has changed her e-mail so many times—from Hotmail to Gmail to RoadRunner—from Katie, to KatieKat, to KTG, to KandMSommers204 (was that her husband?)—

*Oh, wait a minute,* I think. *Facebook.*

I am proud to say I have several thousand friends on Facebook. I'm less proud to admit that this may have less to do with my intrinsic popularity than with Facebook's curious algorithms. Example: while *The Madwoman in the Volvo* was my memoir on menopause, it is most often "liked" by Middle Eastern men brandishing rifles whose names are literally in Arabic. (Is it because they object to a woman driving?)

No matter. I type Katie a personal message: "I'm so humiliated. My dental health is so poor I literally spat a tooth out! I need the sort of dentist who specializes in adult babies in diapers wheeled in hysterical on gurneys! Who's yours? Help!"

After a very carefully chewed (on the right side) early dinner, I return to check the computer. Next turn: in my state of disorientation, instead of sending a private message to Katie, I have somehow managed to post tidings of my rotting mouth to everyone I know on Facebook. We're talking old high school and college friends, professional acquaintances, Goodreads buddies, the Sierra Club, and (if the photos are to be believed) no less than Barack and Michelle Obama.

On the upside? This thread is hu-u-uge, and (*someone is typing . . .* ) growing. It turns out, middle-aged people are really obsessed with their dentists. Within one hour, thirty dentists have been recommended, in locations ranging from Marina del Rey to Rancho Cucamonga, each with its own throaty exhortation ("Ignore the others—you *must* see Dr. Norris!").

As the tsunami of comments grows into the night, my dental emergency starts turning into a kind of dental internet café.

Aside from fascinating details about molars, root canals, and bridgework, there's riffing on the word "tooth"—the whole tooth, nothing but the tooth, you can't handle the tooth, and of course, because I am half Asian: "Chinese dental time—tooth hurty."

Fellow Facebook friends are starting entire side conversations with one another: "David, how can you go to a dentist named Devoree Prepsky?" and "You should talk, yours is Dr. Alma Vilkus-Stockus— what kind of a name is Dr. Alma Vilkus-Stockus?"

There's rapturous discussion of favorite medications—from Valium to Ativan to Tylenol 3, in 2 milligrams, 5 milligrams, 10 milligrams. People go from describing dental emergencies they've endured to posting favorite dentist scenes from movies. These range from Dustin Hoffman being tortured by his Nazi doctor in *Marathon Man* to Tom Conti as a poet with bad teeth in *Reuben, Reuben* to Jack Nicholson as the crazy dental patient in *Little Shop of Horrors*.

At this point, new arrivals are marveling at the very size of the thread. One commentator suggests I dress my piece of tooth in a top hat and a costume, and photograph it like Mr. Peanut. Good God. My tooth has gone viral.

The bottom line: out of all these wonderful L.A. dentists in my brand new Rolodex, I decide I will go with Nan Thompson in Glendale, who "specializes in terror." Even before coming in, I indulge in several phone conversations with the extremely patient Dr. Thompson. Emboldened by all those rantings on Facebook, I utter my "inner monologue" aloud—the first official sign of true middle age, to wit: "I am a fifty-five-year-old person who panics. Sure, I've had children and everything but the dentist is really where I freak out. I hold on to nurses. I grab them. I attack them. You may need to hit me over the head with a frying pan."

She calmly listens as I ruminate and hypothesize about the various ways this could go ("I might jump out of a window"). I doubt eHarmony.com supports this much prescreening.

So Dr. Thompson and I seal the deal. The next day, Charlie drives me. In one of those signature romantic outings of middle age, we have made dual overdue dental appointments.

And let me tell you what a "terror specialist" does. She welcomes you. She seats you. She quietly adjusts the chair while making small talk. Then she says, very gently, "May I look into your mouth?"

Even though a chunk of fairly strange-looking tooth has fallen out and clearly something has gone terribly wrong, instead of screaming, "Good God! It's the worst thing I've seen! The entire mouth is unsaveable!" Dr. Thompson warmly murmurs, without missing a beat, "Nice! Beautiful veneers! And not too many cavities!"

Do you see? This is a dentist with a very low bar. She's saying, "Wow! Look at these! You appear to have teeth! Good job, young lady! You also have a head! Neat!"

In fact, Dr. Thompson is so mellow and friendly and complimentary that it takes totally happy and relaxed me a moment to process her review of my X-ray. To wit: "This may not be the news you want to hear, but due to a split root, infection, and bone loss, we should really extract that tooth."

The "good news" is that an implant will be just $5,000 and quote, unquote: "You'll be buried with it!"

Even better news: "I can pull it out right now."

With novocaine! I balk. *Novocaine.*

Shiver. No can do. Not today.

I pad defeatedly out to the waiting room. Charlie goes in next. He emerges, looking pale. Because we're damaged goods, he too needed a tooth pulled. However, being a cheerful WASP ("I'm unkillable!"), he just went for it, on the spot. His queasy report: "She kind of put her knee on my chest and there was this 'EE ee EE ee EE!' " He makes a squeegee sound and moves clasped hands back and forth as though jacking up a car.

There was no choice but to schedule oral surgery the following Monday and to medicate. I got Valium, Vicodin, and amoxicillin when my (possibly infected?) sinus went temporarily numb.

The night before my procedure, it was a bottle of merlot and the only movie I could stomach, Mel Gibson's *Braveheart.* I felt after three hours of watching raggedy Scots beat the hell out of one another, a simple Glendale tooth extraction would seem like a spa treatment.

And it was. Wow!

I'm thinking of naming my first grandchild "Anesthesia."

And of changing my Facebook relationship status to "In love with Nam Cho, DDS, Oral & Maxillofacial Surgery." But perhaps I'll wait until the pain medication runs out.

# "Winter" Is ~~Coming~~ HERE

## *"January"*

# Welcome to the Jungle (aka: Mice!)

I AM IN A household that's less mixed race or mixed religion than—if this is even a phrase—mixed pest.

My creed? I believe creatures of all types may live in this world. Just not in my kitchen. I pay the mortgage. This is my building. These are my rules. And the first rule is, no ants. If I see a trail on the floor or cluster in the sink, gently swarming, I will grab a Windex bottle and frenetically pump the plastic trigger, spraying the magical blue fluid everywhere, until all is still. Then I'll wipe up the whole mess with paper towels and stuff them in the garbage.

Unfortunately, the human pests—I mean, inhabitants—in my home do not approve.

To begin with, my two daughters, Hannah, fifteen, and Sally, eleven, are idealists. Bossy young idealists. I didn't make my daughters that way—California did. California really is different. It's not just the election that showed us that. California just is. All the jokes are true.

Think of our longtime former leader Jerry Brown. Years ago known as "Governor Moonbeam," that's long over. I don't know how it happened, but once he started losing his hair and not replacing it, Jerry Brown just got older and tougher and more leathery and didn't give a damn, like some dude from the HBO series *Oz*.

Jerry Brown survived a deficit and fires and droughts and Jane Fonda (right?). And so it became "We're California, everyone, f@#$ you!" We're armed with hemp bullet vests, pita chips set on stun.

In Hannah's California public middle school, there was supposed to be a debate about gay marriage, but the teacher couldn't find one student to argue against it. The teens literally couldn't fathom what such an argument would be. Now in high school, Hannah is in the LGBT Club, like all the other cool teens. It's the law, but what she's really become passionate about is the environment. She follows various things about it on Instagram, which I could describe to you if I understood Instagram, or Snapchat (is that still a thing?). Bottom line, the sight of plastic bags makes her nauseated. "People are just so lazy," she says, snapping her gum in disgust. "People are lame."

As am I.

"COMPOST? We don't have a COMPOST?" Hannah exclaimed recently, rolling her eyes.

"Why don't you start by picking up all the old Halloween candy stuck to the floor of your room?" I said. "Or is that some kind of 'compost'? PS: Ants in your 'compost'—have you noticed?"

My fingers itch for my Windex bottle. And roll of *paper towels*. Which Hannah points out is killing both innocent living creatures and forests.

Hannah's younger sister Sally is one of California's disturbing new wave of child vegetarians. I think she caught it from a youthful, pretty vegan yoga teacher who was mysteriously allowed on public school grounds. Although some child vegetarians catch it from the other child vegetarians. It is not because these children like tofu and actual vegetables. Oh no. #secretbacon. The reason for the vegetarianism is always more connected to a vague emotionally upswelling dreamscape. There are misty eyes, there is tearing up. As part of the tale, the sullen overweight family cat is—against his wishes—tightly cradled. It's the same cat that kills birds and leaves them headless on the bathroom floor. The fish feed is, as usual, forgotten. (Never mind that fish eat other fish.)

The bottom line being, Sally refuses to let me kill anything, not even a spider. We're supposed to trap it in a water glass and release it gently into the wild, even if this is a project that takes the greater part of an hour.

And finally, of course, we come to Charlie. Both divorced from our first and only marriages, we've been cohabiting for eight years. We'll leave aside the matter of equality. Yes, because I make more of the money, Charlie theoretically does more of the "housework"— although in practice that's a loosely defined term.

We'll leave aside the fact that ours is the sort of couple where the man believes his woman is neurotic, impatient, and continually over-reacting. Which is to say, I'll observe something with my own eyes—

Perhaps the computer is acting up. A porch bulb has burned out. Flames are coming out of the dishwasher—

And, not even looking up from the *New York Times* food section, Charlie will tell me why what I'm seeing is not possible. (A girlfriend of mine is married to an extremely intelligent, know-it-all paramedic. In her pregnancy's third trimester, she turned to him in the middle of the night and said, "My water broke." Literally in his sleep, he said, "No, it didn't.")

We'll leave aside the fact that Charlie, a Scotch-Irish white-as-the-driven-snow Columbia English major from Evanston, Illinois, is a practicing Hindu. And I don't mean California Lite Eastern Mysticism, where a single "Om" after yoga class is followed by a trip to Whole Foods for kombucha tea. Charlie chants loudly in Sanskrit at home before his little attic altar and attends, without laughing, Hindu fire festivals.

So, re: insects. Charlie (a) doesn't see insects, (b) believes, if they do appear, they have the same karmic rights to exist as us, so (c) no action should be taken as, in any case, they are natural, seasonal, and ebb and flow on their own (he one time asked, "Aren't maggots seasonal?"), and (d) he has this thing about toxic chemicals.

"You're spraying Windex over where we eat!" he'll say. "You're poisoning us!" Fair enough. So over the years, thanks to YouTube and wikiHow—I love wikiHow!—I've developed what I call the Organic Killing Fields.

I've learned how to keep pests at bay in a more healthful and organic manner. For instance, did you know that ants do not like mint or peppermint? So to disinvite them, just smear the threshold of your kitchen door with toothpaste! Do you know "wikiHow" to make a fruit fly trap? Simply take a plastic deli container, fill it with an inch of apple cider vinegar, and jab holes in the top with the sharp tip of a meat thermometer—jab, jab, jab! It's very satisfying.

It's true that when it comes to regular flies, with their teeth-grating buzzing, kindly Sally tries to "dance" them out. I just smack them, hard. My weapon of choice? Forget a fly swatter or a newspaper— that's for amateurs. For size and heft, I've found the perfect fly-killing tool is a rolled-up *New Yorker* magazine, which Charlie has piles of. He won't miss the February 27 issue. Unfortunately, it's so effective I recently broke a window pane. So I now compromise with *AARP Magazine*, which now seems to be omnipresent in our home. I use the one with Dave Matthews on the cover.

ALL OF WHICH is a lengthy backstory to this: recently, during dinner, I get up to go to the kitchen to refill the bread basket. And I see it.

Amid the friendly array of metal bowls, colorful dishes, and moist cutting boards— Across the top of the stove— Across the metal lip that abuts the wall—

A furry gray thing the size of a stick of butter quickly scuttles, right to left. Long stringy tail. To say I scream would be like saying Beyoncé is slightly confident about her body. The family rushes in to support me, as I collapse. "I saw a mouse!" I shrill.

That is a lie. I feel I have actually seen a small rat, due to the tail. But all of this unwelcome data is coming too quickly. And now, of course, with an attentive audience of four, the thing is gone. The rodent has deployed his five-second performance for the exact moment when Nervous Mom entered the kitchen.

"I mean, like a bear, couldn't he hear me coming?" I exclaim. "I'm wearing clogs, for God's sake! Was that *really* the moment to run across the stove?"

As usual, Charlie insists this is not possible. Why? Our house, I should mention, is a large wooden 1906 craftsman with many nooks and crannies. In the honeycombed crawl space below lives a feral cat that we have dubbed "Rico."

"So you can't have seen a mouse," he says.

At which point, I thank God I have a sensible life partner. My Second Husband. Whose name is Angie. Who has a List.

Although, to be honest, when you type the words "rodent control" into Angie's List it's a little horrifying. Word of advice, to pest control people. In selecting images to advertise your business, we're already a bit freaked out by the grisly details. Think of the gentle artistry of feminine hygiene ads, or Viagra ads. Help us out with feel-good metaphors. We want to see a woman in pink capri pants skipping joyously through a field, or an attractive silver-haired couple chuckling in side-by-side soak tubs in wine country.

For "rodent control" companies, a reassuring image might include a smiling family in matching cardigans enjoying a candlelit picnic on their living room floor. Or perhaps a mom in shorty shorts lolling on that same floor eating Triscuits and reading O Magazine— Think, essentially, *people not afraid to come in contact with their floors*, as opposite to me, who now traverses my home by hopping as though electrocuted, with my hands over my eyes, screaming "No! No! No!"

No such luck. Scrolling through the ads and coupons, I see intimate color close-ups of rats and mice, with reddish eyes, shiny noses, and trembling whiskers, either outside, gazing victoriously to the sky, Willard-like, or, most memorably, on a cheese plate. That's right. I see a furry, sparkly-eyed rodent slyly turning to us—essentially, photo bombing—an otherwise tasty-looking cheese plate.

But, oh! To its right, there's a 30 percent-off coupon for "live animal trapping." I click on it, cinch my spa robe belt, cross my fingers.

THE VERY NEXT DAY, a pest control specialist comes to my house. He is a youthful tattooed man in blue coveralls named Fabian, whose narrow facial features, truth be told, make him look himself like a mouse. Fabian finds mouse droppings under the sink, indicating that we do indeed have rodents.

I'm elated! Until now, I was the only person in my house who thought I saw a mouse. This means I am not crazy!

My elation fades when I learn Fabian-the-pest-control-guy's plan.

It's true that I am not an expert in getting rid of rodents. I guess I was vaguely hoping for some kind of computer-driven laser beam or humane technology involving sonic waves. (SLEEP THRU DENTISTRY!) But no. Fabian is now trundling in an old-fashioned wooden mousetrap, with the gnarly metal spring, two big white glue boards, and, yes . . . a jar of Skippy peanut butter. Creamy style.

Under the stove the glue boards go. We can call Fabian when we catch something. Nothing happens, day after day, so we assume that the mouse simply ran back outside. Then Friday noon, I'm eating a salad, in my home office, and to my disbelief, I see, just a few feet in front of me, a small gray shivering fur ball. It's a tiny baby mouse, the size of my thumb, plodding around in methodical circles, looking confused, on the shaggy IKEA rope rug under the computer table where I work. Oh my God.

I put my salad down and look for a bucket.

All I can find is a fancy hexagonal gift box full of bath bombs from the cosmetics store Lush. I empty the box in a whoosh of lavender dust and approach the tottering baby mouse. I am making high-pitched screaming sounds in my head.

I try to upend the box over the mouse. But he(?) suddenly develops some unexpected thinking skills and eludes me, darting behind the piano. I close the pocket doors of the office and call Fabian. He tells me to transfer one of the glue traps under the stove to the living room.

Now, I am a proud feminist, but to me, this all falls under a category called "MAN." So when Charlie comes home twenty minutes later, I assign him to it. Charlie ducks down to pull a glue trap out from under the stove and says, "Whoa." Never a good sign. One of the glue traps is already occupied by a larger dead mouse. Oh God. The word "infestation" is flashing across my brain pan.

He picks up the second glue trap. I open the pocket doors to the office. From out of nowhere, the baby mouse darts toward him—my mind flashes to the killer bunny in that Monty Python movie.

Charlie screams—that's a first for him. I swiftly close the doors.

"He's just sitting here, looking at me," Charlie narrates, in growing disbelief. "He's not that smart. Whoa! He just came up and sniffed the trap! He was an inch away!"

"This is horrible!" I exclaim, now actually envisioning the mouse baby's slow gluey death. It's so very opposite of *Ratatouille*, or any other Disney movie.

I open a door and hand Charlie the fancy hexagonal gift box from Lush. He upends the perfumey pink box over the mouse. Under it he slides a record recently pressed by his tirelessly productive indie musician friend Tex. "Vinyl, man, 'everyone's' going back to vinyl," Tex said. How very true. Particularly when "everyone" has rodents.

Charlie carries the baby mouse outside and releases it. As we are just ten feet away from where Rico the feral cat lives, we're essentially a meal delivery service. But at least we won't witness actual violence.

The next night, Sally, Charlie, and I have made a fortress of pillows on our bed upstairs, enjoying Sally's current favorite show *Supernatural*. All of a sudden, she exclaims, "Oh no, look!"

And, at our bedroom door, on the second floor, another baby mouse! Staring at us!

"This is a big house!" I yell. "This mouse could go anywhere! We are three humans shrieking aloud in fear as we watch a very noisy TV show about ghosts and demons. Shouldn't mice be scared off by the sound? Like bears?"

Charlie and Sally grab the Lush bath bomb box, slide another of Tex's indie records under it (it's suddenly nice we have so many of them) and carry the mouse downstairs, with the plan to, as usual, liberate it onto the front porch. But at the bottom porch stair, the baby mouse, who managed to get up twenty-five stairs with absolutely no problem, does a belly flop onto the concrete and stops moving, stone-cold dead. Sally begins wailing. Gawd! It's like a horror show!

I put my arms around her to comfort her, and . . . what? These are the Parent/Child Conversational Moments where I literally have no idea what to say. My usual route is to immediately go meta-philosophical, changing the topic so entirely that I confuse the child. I follow that up with simple lying.

"It's just, honey— Don't be sad! You understand that babies aren't fully cooked yet, brain development-wise. They need several months to actually become individuals. Think human babies. Mice babies. Kittens. Oh, remember at our other house, when we had those oceans of feral black kittens. Furry, blinking, cute . . ."

*And hell-bent on suicide*, I now horribly remember. These seemed to be their tiny trains of thought: "Swimming pool? Let's jump in! Who's next door? Pitbulls! Yay! Can we run faster than this car? Apparently, no! Splat."

So I just skipped the talk and pulled out ice cream. Rocky Road *and* Elephant Tracks. It seemed fitting.

"February"

Rebirthing Shoots
of Grass in the Ice

"cheese therapy"

# Pema Bollywood/The Goddess Within/Fifty-Sixth Birthday/ My Goddess, Myself

MAYBE IT'S BECAUSE every time "Miracle Cure for Belly Fat!" appears on my computer screen, I click on it. Maybe it's the suite of Pandora stations I've created—"jazz flute," "soothing solo piano," and yes, no apologies, "James Taylor."

Fact is, the algorithms have found me—a middle-aged lady with a VISA card! So through every device now I'm being pelted with ads for "Christian singles over 50," colorful plus-sized "Zulily" clothing, Zoloft, Cedars-Sinai arthroscopic knee surgery (the male announcer is so soothing I'm tempted to just *have* the surgery), and even . . . promotional e-mails from life coaches eager to help fifty-something me become both a *bold warrioress* and a *joyful goddess.* Recent example:

*Hello Beautiful Sandra Loh,*
  *I want to help you break through the things that are holding you back so you can create more of the life you want and less of the life you don't want, now!*
  *We'll work together to:*

*Clarify what you want to change*
*Foster self care*
*Honor your inner "no"*
*Bloom into your True Self*
*Find joy, joy, joy!*


*Beautiful Sandra Loh, welcome to Goddesshood!*


SURE, WHEN WE were in our thirties, I suggested to my sister that as we got older and our ages became emotionally unwieldy, I could just give her a cake that said, "Happy Goddess Day!" on it. To which she said, "If you ever do that, I will kill you first and then I will kill myself."

But really. What's so wrong with the goddess thing? It is my birthday. That's right.

After everything horrible that's happened in our country and on our planet, more welcome news. I'm turning fifty-six! I'm now closer to sixty than fifty. Gah! What's to celebrate?

I mean, by fifty-six, I've had career ups and downs. I have kids, a partner, and a house. In the main, I am fine. At this point, no single phone call is going to radically change my life, except for medical tests results, and those are not likely to be fantastic. ("Congratulations! You're pregnant!" "Our scanner reveals that you have magically lost seventeen pounds!" or "We've literally found a million dollars inside of your body!")

I'm trying to imagine what I'm going to become next. I've been a twentysomething ingénue, thirtysomething career girl, fortysomething mom, fiftysomething . . . what? Dame? Matron? Queen Mother? (Bella Abzug?)

Why not goddess?

Why not silvery goddess?

SUNDAY EVENINGS ARE not pretty. First, I think Sally is acting out because at 8:30 sharp I snapped off her TV show—always a traumatic event.

But no, the wailing continues over the fact that—of course—she *hates all her pants*. I have inadvertently dissed some of her stuffed animals by facing them in the wrong direction. She also misses her dad.

On the phone to him, as I wait just outside her door with her hot chocolate, Sally rails on and on about her miseries, in an escalating pitch, until finally, in real alarm, Ben asks, "Did something *happen* today?"

And out it comes, her youthful cri de coeur: "I HATE MONDAYS!"

"Well, everyone hates Mondays," I say afterward, rubbing her skinny shoulders. "In winter, BLUE MONDAY is said to be the most depressing day of the year. It's part the dark weather, part time elapsed since Christmas, part failing one's New Year's resolutions. God, now even I'm getting depressed."

Her face still in her hands, Sally cracks a little smile.

So she can still be comforted, at least temporarily. But sometimes I worry about these huge storms of feeling that come over her. It's not just her stuffed animals. She will weep over a seashell broken in a box. Or a snapped bird feather. When she was eight, a toothpaste cap disappeared down the bathroom sink drain. Wailed Sally, "That toothpaste cap was my best friend!"

Hannah, thank God, is the rock.

But the next day during lunch, Hannah texts me from school.

**Mom, please pick up. I thought I aced my test in AP World History but I bombed it. I've dropped to a low C. I'm so scared and sad. ;(**

Until now, Hannah has always sailed through school. But now that it's sophomore year, she has three AP classes and it's the first time her GPA actually counts. It's like her grades are pinging around in a pinball machine, hitting every different letter of the alphabet. Plus her sleep/study habits seem like they were birthed in a jungle. Every morning at 5:30 a.m., when we have to get up, I find Hannah dead asleep, face smashed into her open history book, earphones still blasting (death metal—still even a thing?).

Having apparently missed her, I now call and call and she doesn't answer. When I pick Hannah up after school, with great purring empathy, I ask whether we should resume EdLine—where parents have online access to their children's grades. "Hell no!" Hannah says, completely refreshed, and reconfident. It's like she has forgotten her woes already. "Wallace is allowing me extra credit, and so is Ms. Said in chemistry, which brings my GPA up to a 3.75."

"Oh!" I exclaim. This is the first I've heard a GPA of any number.

"Uh-huh," Hannah says, more obliquely. With an almost reptilian blink of her yellow-shadowed eyes (yellow? is that some Japanese thing?), the portals close again. It sometimes feels like my fifteen-year-old is auditioning multiple personalities on me. She's alternately sassy, then vulnerable, then needy, then secretive . . . and I, her mom, am always one wrong step behind in the cycle.

Which is to say, between these two girls, I'm shell-shocked every day. The waves of their emotions batter against me. But I have to be a calm mom. I feel I literally have to not spasm, to keep my body soft.

As the Goddess Project says, to heal pain points: "Ice to water, water to vapor. Ohhhhm."

Julia calls—she wants me to join her in a 6 p.m. Groupon cardio barre class.

*Cardio barre.*

Goddess-like, I dig within my True Self and find . . . the inner no!

IN THE MAIL, I get a catalogue from a company called Softer Seasons and I like it. I like it a lot. It features serene women of a certain age smiling secretively to themselves as they move glamorously alone through gauzy abodes. There is:

A single wine glass holder for personal tub soaking. (Note: nothing is for two.)

A kind of bathrobe/kimono that—it's hard to explain— looks like you can take it on or off in one simple tie.

A pashmina blanket—wait, no, Snuggie—a specialized Snuggie for people who apparently find regular Snuggies too complicated.

I love all of it. From now on, I want everything around me to be soft. I buy a discounted pillow from Target that says, SWEATPANTS ZONE. Also, socks just for the house, fuzzy socks.

I see walk-in tubs advertised in *AARP Magazine* and think, *What a great idea!*

I CONTINUE MAKING online forays into goddesshood, from a menu of options that come to resemble a kind of Angie's List, if you will, of personal transformation. This voyage does not proceed entirely smoothly.

I do a five-minute online meditation. It's a video of a peaceful forest, with Tibetan bell sounds, but I'm bothered by a faint buzzing sound in the background. Is that a chainsaw?

I try an online webinar in goddess energy. The goddess energy is, unfortunately, being summoned from a rather dingy looking attic. Louise Wellman, the webinar leader, an addled older lady with a shock of gray hair, is having a lot of technical problems. "Is it on?" she keeps murmuring, in her trance voice. "I think the camera's on now. A red light is blinking. Isn't it?" But we can only see her from eyebrows up.

I study an online brochure for a seventy-two-hour women's spiritual retreat. I am tempted—the surrounding countryside looks gorgeous. But it's hard to figure out whether the cabins are nice or dumpy. There are one too many enigmatic close-ups of hands reaching out to plates of fussily arranged fruit. There are one too many soft-lit photos of lumpy women in sweatpants with closed eyes, holding hands in a circle.

Where is the wine—?

Ah— Possibly no wine, because the retreat is about "women's emotional healing, addiction recovery, trauma relief, personal transformation, midlife reinvention."

This sounds too intense. I'm breaking into a sweat just thinking about it. Ice to water, water to vapor.

I think I'm going to have to do this goddess thing my way. Sort of an à la carte thing. Compare goddess fabric swatches. I drive to the Third Eye Bookstore I've always been curious about, in South Pasadena. VISA card in hand, I strike gold. Granted, at first I get a little snarled in the Wiccan section. I'm visually drawn to a "Know Your Elves" calendar with daily magickal practices. But as I page through it, I realize there are too many kinds of elves—wood ones and air ones and water ones. It requires too much constant gardening of little herb pots and then buying special stones like lapis lazuli to place into the little pots. Instead of "self-care," it is "elf care."

I pick up another book: *The Warrior Goddess Way: Clarity, Creativity, and Inner Power for Women—Birth a Path of Authenticity and Honesty.* Blood red cover. No.

But look: here's *The Pocket Pema Chödrön* that fits into a felted saddle bag with a peace sign, 40 percent off! A tarot deck . . . totally made of cats! "I love it!" I hear myself crow. An essential oil (chamomile, frankincense) car air freshener! Something called *The Green Goddess Cookbook*, featuring stunning sunlit photos of olive oil, peaches, soft cheeses, and—look at this sultry chapter title: "A Passion for Ramps." *Ramps!* I think, shimmying my deliciously plump shoulders. "A Passion for Ramps!"

I see an Ayurvedic Goddess Massage advertised and, while it's pricey, for my birthday, I book it! Then I turn the corner, and there it is: the Himalayan tie-dye section. The colorful drapey hangers invite and fling their musliny arms out to me. And I see them: blossomy purple harem pants, in a style I might call "Pema Bollywood."

I look at the tag and see those four magical words: "One Size Fits All."


My birthday always falls around the time of Mardi Gras.

A rabid New Orleans lover, Charlie always observes Mardi Gras. However, Mardi Gras is a very hard party to throw. "Fat Tuesday" is also always a big fat school night. Anyway, most of our friends in L.A. think Mardi Gras is kind of weird, like some kind of skanky Bourbon Street boob-flashing thing. As opposed to having deep mystical/Native American/Zulu tribal roots, according to Charlie.

So, in the past couple of years on Mardi Gras, Charlie has started

having just three friends over who I've dubbed "the Gentlemen Callers."
Let me describe them to you this way. Picture a yin/yang symbol of
polar opposites. If on the left, Sheryl Sandberg and her flotilla of Type A
female leaders are leaning *in* in snappy A-line skirts, to the right, Charlie and his brethren are leaning *out*, in colorful dashikis and tinfoil hats.

Which is to say, theirs is an artisanal (aged in small batches)
definition of maleness.

These brethren all met at Columbia in the late 1970s, when you
could practically get in with a C average. (A simpler time, Charlie
wrote his AP English essay on a work of literature he totally made up
called "Apartment House Raga.") The Gentlemen studied everything
arcane and fascinating and useless, from English to erotic Japanese
statuary to eighteenth-century horticulture. Passions include Hinduism, Sun Ra, Afrofuturism, vinyl, free jazz, and home cannabis delivery. You may also see antique globe collections, matchbook collections,
and, hanging above a snarl of out-of-tune electric guitars, a broken
tin whistle. By day they make small livings (manager of an apartment
building, used-books seller, freelance luthier), not typically discussed.

The Gentlemen have a swath of put-upon wives and girlfriends.
Many of us are on the spectrum—we are science fiction novelists,
library scientists, oboe professors. Financially independent, we suffer our Gentlemen's eccentricities and fiduciary problems, because,
unlike many alpha males with real jobs, they are amusing company.

So, celebrating Mardi Gras here today are:

> Tex, Hawaiian shirts, has some family mystery money,
>     collects vinyl.
> Jerry, Utilikilts, has a professional background in dance,
>     mime, and clowning. Jerry married very well, to that gal
>     on TV who plays the astrophysicist on that thing (one of
>     the *Star Treks*?).

Bradford writes opera librettos. I have to say, Bradford
has really blown up over the years. He is now almost
obese, but never not in a blazer, the buttons practically
popping off. But he is happy with himself. As he has said
comfortably, stretching his arms out: "I am a perfect size
fifty-two."

All four Gentlemen, including Charlie, have lived, at various
times, in New Orleans. (Most went to Burning Man once, but were
too lazy to go a second time.) They all understand Mardi Gras, the
history, the legacy, the various parade "krewes."

So here it is, 2 p.m. in the afternoon. WWOZ New Orleans is
streaming from the big living room computer. Charlie is standing in
the kitchen, drinking a Bloody Mary and swirling a roux.

Tex is texting his NOLA musician buddies to see what's going on.
"They're at St. Ann's now!" he calls out. "With Jewlu!"

Bradford is unpacking bags of essential NOLA ingredients: "I
had to drive all the way to Altadena to find the Crystal hot sauce.
And pickled okra. And of course we'll need Peychaud's Bitters"—he
waves a bottle—"for the Sazeracs."

Jerry is "warming up" by doing tai chi on the back deck.

On one of my four-time-a-week shopping rounds, I've picked up
Mardi Gras beads at the Van Nuys Party Store. Charlie refuses them
for their inauthenticity. Truth be told, the gold, green, and pink just
looks tinny and sad. The plastic bags sit on the back porch unopened.
More successful is the authentic King Cake I've bought, somehow
effortlessly executed by Porto's Armenian Bakery in Glendale. And
for a time, all is festive. Cocktails clank, gumbo is engorged, Jerry
and Charlie spar—with (relative) good humor—about the correct
way to turn the shrimp on the barbecue. Charlie and Jerry always
fight about the barbecue. This segues into drunken bro dancing in

the backyard to a Cajun beat and singing that sounds like "Hey now! Hey now! Hey now! Hey now! Waikowaikowaiko!"

Mid-dance line, Charlie is seized with a brilliant idea: "I'm going to drive my VW beetle to Louisiana and register it! No smog laws there! Who's in?"

"Road . . . trip!" everybody cheers. Never mind that the Beetle, with all the junk in it, at best seats three and can barely get to Long Beach.

The first pall comes upon Tex's announcement that by 11 in New Orleans, 9 p.m. our time, second lines are breaking out all over town.

Charlie's eyes glitter with joy—and then he takes the dark turn. "God, Mardi Gras in New Orleans is the best party on earth and every year I miss it!"

"And who knows how long New Orleans is even going to be there," Bradford helpfully adds, downing another Sazerac. "What with global warming—"

"The levees, the flooding," Jerry agrees.

"Thanks to the great almighty US of A!" Tex adds.

And oh boy, here we go, where so many of these gatherings eventually do . . . into the howling pit of political ranting. Which gives liberty to much shouting and bellicosity and the mad chain-smoking of American Spirit cigarettes (who brought those?).

"If it hadn't been for the Russians—!"

"The Republican base—!"

"The Christian Right—!"

"Gerrymandering—!"

"The oil industry—!"

"Dark money—!"

"Big pharma—!"

"Coal—!"

My sphincter seizes up with it all! I can't stand it!

. . .

SATURDAY MORNING, when I come out in my fabulous purple Pema Bollywood goddess pants, my household is not impressed.

Wisecracks Charlie (whose Mardi Gras hangover is finally lifting): "Did a clown die?" Sassy with mystery extra credit, Hannah mimes handing me a phone: "The eighties called. They want their pants back."

"No problem," I say grandly to all of them, embracing my inner size fifty-two. "I'm going to forgive all of you, because my birthday today is all about self-celebration."

I'm doing that by throwing a simple birthday brunch. With ground rules. To begin with, conversationally, this one day will be a politics-free zone. It's a safe space. A very soft, safe space.

I've asked all my girlfriends to bring any one of "the three C's"— champagne, chocolate, or cheese. Just in case there is not *enough* cheese, I've stockpiled it. Right next to the Third Eye Bookstore I found a store called "cheese therapy" (all lower case, upper case being too stressful in these difficult times). It has its own "mac-and-cheese" bar, which includes gluten-free mac and dairy-free cheese (South Pasadena is a very particular town). Having no dietary limitations myself, I've rounded up a bunch of high-fat goddess food. A fontina-artichoke-honey dip. Camembert with cranberries. Brie and peaches.

On the big living room computer: Joni Mitchell.

"What is this?" Julia wrinkles her nose as she walks in, still clutching her gift bag. "*Ladies of the Canyon?*"

"Are we officially out of our *Blue* years now?" Andie asks. "Or *Court and Spark?*"

"*Ladies of the Canyon*, yes, suckas!" I say. "I'm now on Malibu time. Get used to it. I'm going to wear a wind-blown scarf and drive alone up the coast in a vintage convertible and I *will* paint breezy seascapes."

"Okay," Julia and Andie say, exchanging glances.

"PS," I say, "I know I often make everyone throw the I-Ching on my birthday, but I'm sick of it. There's too much darkness there—'The Abyss,' 'Biting Through,' 'The Preponderance of the Small.' Those Chinese can be tough. One time I had an eighty-year-old feng shui guy come to my old house and he said my then husband Ben would die in five years of a head injury. So today we're saging that energy out and working with this very nice tarot deck card of white cats. I've taken all the bad cards out, like 'Death' and 'The Tower.' "

What happens next reminds me that maybe I need to get new girlfriends.

I always have this idea that I'm going to get together with My Girlfriends and that it will be fun and fabulous. Sort of like on *Sex and the City*, or like with Nora Ephron and her I'm pretty sure fabulous girlfriends (Rosie O'Donnell?). Or Oprah, as on *Oprah After the Show*. I am fifty-six. These are supposed to be the Oprah/Gayle chill years, of Northern Californian spa retreats, hot stone massages, coconut oil, wealth.

"What are you doing?" Andie asks.

"You have a 'cat' tarot deck . . . and you've taken out the difficult cards?" Julia asks.

"It's my personal journey to goddesshood!" I exclaim.

Thank God now my more woo-woo girlfriend Marilyn arrives, in dark glasses and a sunbrella hat, clutching what seems like a Jeroboam of Honest Tea.

Marilyn puts her hand up.

"No alcohol. I am on . . . A. Forty-eight-hour. Sugar. Cleanse."

We all murmur how great that is—

Although I can't help thinking, at the rate Marilyn goes on sugar cleanses—I mean, how much sugar is Marilyn ingesting that she needs such frequent cleansing? The last time it was a 72-hour cleanse. Now it's 48 hours. Soon it will be "I'm going on a 4-hour sugar cleanse." Does that mean the other 20 hours of the day sugar is being bolted?

Julia—she of the unwanted Groupon cardio barre—returns to what is becoming an attack.

"I don't know what you're doing with these—these *pants*, but Sandra, honey, these are *not* the Eileen Fischer years!"

"Um, excuse me," I lash back, stung. "I'm fifty-six. I believe these *are* the Eileen Fischer years. In fact, starting from age twenty-two, I kind of wanted them *all* to be the Eileen Fischer years!"

Marilyn nods sagely, quaffing her Honest Tea.

"That's right. Yes. This is the time of the important 'crone' work."

"God, no!" Andie wails. She is mysteriously rearranging the cheeses. What—is there a more "correct" order? Alphabetical?

" 'Crone,' really?" Julia exclaims. She herself is dressed in a tailored white shirt today, and cuffed stylish jeans.

"Crone, yes," I say to Marilyn. "I love that idea. Instead of bemoaning the fact that I don't have the skin of a twenty-six-year-old, I can look in the mirror and say, 'Wow! Look at that! I have pretty great skin for a CRONE!' "

"Yes," Marilyn says, smearing brie and peaches on a baguette. "It's very important work."

"You know what they say, 'When I am an old woman, I shall wear purple!' " I exclaim, throwing my arm out like a badass Lady of the Canyon.

Julia puts both hands on my shoulders: "I'm sorry, Sandra," she says, "but you're not quite that old yet. We've got Madonna. Jane Fonda. Even Betty White. No one is wearing purple."

"What about Golda Meir?" Marilyn asks, waving her brie to the wind.

"Come on, people!" I exclaim. "I'm tired of trying to be young! Why should I even have fitness goals anymore? Every time, I get really excited about a Groupon 'bikini boot camp' thing with rock-hard pecs and six-pack abs, but four weeks later I'm burned out over that nonsense. I've repeated this cycle a zillion times! When do I get to give up?"

"You've got to use it or lose it," Andie says.

"If I make it to my eighties?" I push on. "You're supposed to *gain* weight. That's right. Things flip. If your blood pressure rises, it's better for your mental alertness."

"Have you heard about Renee?" Julia asks, eyebrows up. "She's sixty-eight and winning surfing competitions—huge spread in *AARP* magazine—"

"Yeah, *maybe* when I'm sixty I'll get the short fabulous silver hair and I'll start training for half marathons!" I'm practically yelling now. "But the back half of the fifties are the readjustment years. Hashtag Menopause. Isn't this time for a pause?"

"So true," Marilyn says with a nod. "My daughter Clare signed me up for this gym, but the classes are so confusing. If you come in sneakers, everyone's barefoot. If you come barefoot, everyone's in sneakers. Finally, I found my grail: 'Cardio-Broadway!' I was all set to do 'Wilkommen, bienvenue!' from *Cabaret*. But no. This was all about *Kinky Boots* and *Hamilton*. Who has time to fly to New York to see that?"

"And all that yo-yo dieting," I say, slathering peach/brie on my Costco baguette so vigorously I feel sure it will count as cardio. "Sure, I can deny myself for weeks, doing only the nonfat Greek yogurt, anorexic chicken breast (don't you feel like even the organic chickens, now, are anorexic?), the—blech!—steamed broccoli. But now that my children are no longer toddlers on my lap at Chuck E. Cheese's,

with that horrible wine grotto— One of the boons of middle age is
that my divorced partner and I can Yelp some new gastro bistro and
see a frisée of salad topped with a gleaming fried duck egg or pasta
with pancetta and white truffle oil. Even with a Tuesday Groupon,
no one can afford this but people over forty-five, so if we don't eat
it, who else will? The *New York Times* food section always has big
pieces on how to make your own pasta, and I'm thinking 'Who under
the age of forty-five is reading this, and who still gets to eat pasta?'"

"Heh heh, I know," Andie suddenly says. "The other day I actually thought 'In order to eat fried chicken, I'm going to have to mur-
der someone, go to trial with poor legal representation, end up on
death row, and only *then* will I allow myself to order a last meal of
fried chicken."

"Why would I want to be young again?" I ask, sawing like a
Viking into the Camembert with cranberries. "God! Just look at
what my girls are going through! They have to get up at the armpit
of hell called 5:30 a.m. At 6:30 a.m. in the inky blackness, Sally
pushes open the chiming car door and wails, 'Ohhhhh! We have to
run today. Timed miles!' The last time Sally joined hands with two
classmates and exclaimed, 'For Narnia!' before the buzzer went off,
she ran a six-minute mile and threw up! Jesus!

"And that," I say, chawing on my baguette, "*that* is the fantastic thing about being middle-aged. I'll never have to do an exercise I
don't want to do ever again."

"How about a personal trainer?" Julia asks.

"Oh," I say. "A couple of years ago, I stupidly paid a personal
trainer to make me do things I didn't want to do, ever. Stephanie
would say things like, 'Do ten burpees' and I would actually try to do
them. Idiot. You know what I would say now, at age fifty-six? I would
say, 'You want me to do a burpee? You're fired.' Or better yet, 'You
want me to do a burpee? I'm notifying my attorney, ophthalmologist,

dermatologist, and anesthesiologist and I'm having *them* fire you. I'm unleashing my inner Leona Helmsley."

"Honey," Julia says, "you have to keep evolving. You have to keep trying new things!"

"Things that are new now blow," I tell her. "For instance, last winter, Charlie's family invited me to join them on a 'fun ski day' in Vermont. Did I know how to ski? Technically, yes, I last skied when I was eight, which felt recent, although in fact—and that is the continual amazement of midlife—that was actually like a hundred years ago.

"This became clear when I was handed a pair of modern ski boots. A typical ski boot used to have laces. This thing was like a pressurized canister that used gravity to swallow my foot whole, causing hydraulic bolts to snap shut around my chubby calf, making it feel like it was being Skilsawed in two. Upon being handing skis and poles and a helmet, I realized I couldn't walk. Forty minutes into my ski adventure, like a beached whale, I literally couldn't get out of the building.

"It was then that I first put on what I call my 'ski face.' All around me were pod people behaving as though skiing was a perfectly normal—even fun—activity. I alone knew it was not. The most sensible course of action was to lie down on the dirty carpet next to the hot chocolate machine, crying, so a team of Army engineers could chopper in and unspring me from my cruel leg traps. And yet, maybe the skiers would turn on me if they smelled fear. I would pretend calm and enjoyment, even though I had no idea in what direction the slopes were or what on earth I would do when I found them.

"But me on skis is not great either. Instead of a skill level of five or four, I'm like a minus ten, meaning I need a team of sherpas not just to carry me up the hill but to push me out of the way of actual skiers.

"Even getting to the bottom of the bunny slope seemed impossible. How do you walk uphill in skis? I kept sliding backward and careening into other people, including some five-year-olds. Fortunately, all five-year-olds are excellent skiers—a Lilliputian team of them helpfully pushed me toward the rope tow.

"The attendant handed the rope tow to me. I grabbed it, but it jerked forward with surprising strength and I was literally now being dragged spread eagle forward over the snow. It's amazing how many things can go wrong so quickly. Later I do a face-splat off a chair lift—they actually have to shut the whole thing down for ten minutes. Bottom line: snow is not fun!"

"What are you going to do?" Andie asks. "Just stop trying and quit?"

"Why not?" I exclaim. "Can't I step out of the endless cycle of self-improvement? Which is"—here a new idea strikes me—"itself a form of capitalism, isn't it? Marilyn! Help me out."

"What on earth are you talking about?" Julia asks.

"Yes—the capitalization of feminism," Marilyn says, twirling her baguette in the brie. "To whip women into a bipolar frenzy of dependence on purchasing outside products to 'fix' us, the pattern is 'Chastise! Indulge!' It's all 'Lose ten pounds!' "

I riff back to her:

"Here's a scrumptious fudge brownie recipe your family will love!"

"Walk off the belly fat in thirty days!"

"Oprah says, 'Love and accept yourself for WHO YOU ARE.' Buy the book!"

"You may not have noticed, but YOUR HAIRSTYLE IS AGING YOU!!!"

"Indulge in some hazelnut Dove Bars immediately. Order online. Two-hour delivery."

"Depressed and confused? Try Cymbalta."

"Are your toes ugly? The twenty-minute pedicure."

"Practice Kegels—"

"I know," I say, "even the vagina. It's not enough that it stretches to give birth. Now it has to stay slim and thoughtful and moisturized. It's another thing on the to-do list. Jesus! Isn't fifty-six an age where I don't have to do this anymore? Can't my vagina just take a smoke break and do crosswords now? Can't it just be an obese, retired Nancy Pelosi who goes to Las Vegas and gambles?"

"Honey," Andie says. "It's just that for you, 'goddesshood' seems to be just about eating cheese and not exercising!"


No MATTER IF my girlfriends don't get it. Or if the party ends without anyone even touching my adorable fanned-out "cat" tarot cards.

The next morning is my personal time to shine.

I go into Third Eye, for my magical 11 a.m. "shirodhara" goddess massage. It is a physically and spiritually transformative eighty-minute Ayurvedic massage treatment, whose culmination is warm oil poured soothingly onto your third eye. ("You have to experience it to believe it," enthuse, on the website, apparently rejuvenated clients.)

I sit in the waiting room in my fluffy spa robe, sipping lemon cucumber water. Therapists come out and greet their clients. At 10:58. 11:00. 11:03. 11:05. While waiting, I can only laugh watching my monkey mind count the minutes. So what if it's six minutes after 11? Now seven. The door opens—there she is! Vasti!

Vasti gently leads me to our treatment room and sits me on the massage table. Indicating a basket of oils, she asks, gently, "Are you familiar with Ayurveda? With the three doshas? Vata, Pitta, Kapha?"

I tend to not like eighty-minute—and now due to the lateness, seventy-three-minute—massages that begin with an enervating

Ayurvedic lecture. Never mind. Deep breathing. Om. I quickly select the oil that smells nicest, like a vanilla lymph node. And she begins.

Although there is much fussy, almost ritual draping and redraping going on, it's a nice massage and I relax. It's true that the room has a space heater, the bed warmer is on, we're in a California winter heat wave, and I am fifty-six. But—

Whoa! What's this? A drizzle of—ouch—almost scorching oil splattering onto my forehead. Then oozing into my scalp and eyebrows—eww—

I endure this, biting my lip, so transformation can happen, but forty seconds in I am forced to ask, "How long does this go on for?"

"Eight minutes."

I sit up, pulling my sheet around myself in shame. I've failed at Ayurveda—and the bar was low! "Stop it!" I shrill.

"No problem," she says calmly, rebundling my head in yet another towel, before retreating. "I'll leave you for your five minutes of personal time."

Fully refreshed, I arise from shirodhara ready to do what stressed middle-aged ladies do best. I yell at the front desk and demand a discount. They give me 30 percent off—which I guess is for the third eye, so we'll call it even.

# Home Self-Care

THE TIME HAS COME. I can deny it no longer.
My three-story 1906 craftsman house has become a haunted house–like eyesore. Understand that we live in a historic enclave in Pasadena called Greenfield Heights whose local pride—fueled by architectural tours and block parties and wine tastings—only continues to swell. Yesterday, right across the street, on our neighbor's lawn, a fussy GREEN GARDENING AWARD sign went up. The arrow was conspicuously pointing toward his lawn, away from ours.

Further, our most recent Greenfield Heights e-newsletter said, under a banner titled NEIGHBORHOOD PRIDE: "Please e-mail us if you need references for gardening, painting, or deck refinishing." Was this for my eyes only? Back in 2009, at the bottom of the market, I bought my home on a short sale. I can't explain exactly what that means, except to say, as the owners were in trouble, I got the house way below market value. Yay! Unfortunately, it was not enough below market value that I had money left over to properly maintain it. So it's basically fallen, like Norman Bates's house, into disrepair.

However, here's what my *Pocket Pema Chödrön* says: "You can feel as wretched as you like, and you're still a good candidate for enlightenment."

So starting today, I'm going to be newly proactive about my house problems, which are many.

## BAD FRONT YARD

When I first bought this house, the grass was green. Our new gardener Vic—who seemed to immediately materialize out of a hedge—was a genius at setting sprinkler timers. The lawns looked great and then we got our first—? Well, it was less a water "bill" than a water citation. Water tirade. Water hazing. Our utility company began mailing us accusing bar graphs showing what hogs we were compared to our (far superior) neighbors.

So, in response to the drought emergency declared by Jerry Brown, we decided to let the lawn turn the color of the governor's name. It was a badge of honor. A few years went by. I became increasingly short-tempered. First I thought it was menopause. Then one day, I realized it was because our gardener Vic was coming every Saturday morning at 8 a.m. With a high-pitched, shrieking machine, he would blow dead leaves around our brown yard for an hour. The ear-splitting sound was no doubt meant to prove that he was busy "gardening."

It took another two years for me to let him go. The irony was that I would have kept paying him to simply stop leaf blowing, but having a diligent work ethic (or perhaps a secret love of ear-splitting leaf blowing?), he refused.

That said, I would still like to apologize to our neighbors, block, zip code—really, to everyone, in Los Angeles—less for our front "lawn" than what is now a rectangle of compacted dirt. Our small Okie Dust Bowl is actually dangerous due to the heavy dead palm fronds that intermittently plunge from the sky like Damoclean swords. I want to throw a sheet over our front yard, like a corpse! Or at least put up a sign that says, WE KNOW, WE KNOW. AND WE'RE SORRY!

## PAINTERS

If only home reno was as a simple as on HGTV's *Fixer Upper*, which I'm obsessed with. In it, toothsome Texans Chip and Joanna Gaines will show an anxious couple three falling-down houses. The couple picks one. I love how easy Chip and Joanna make it. The couple says what their personalities are like—she says: "I'm a homebody. He's outdoorsy." Chip and Joanna proceed with sledgehammers, tearing off the "ship lap," repainting it cobalt, and festooning it with design elements from Joanna's handy online store—stainless steel fixtures, antique farm lamps, adorable distressed-wood flower boxes. Two months later the couple returns to a landscaped backyard terrace that magically "brings the outdoors in" with a throw pillow that says NATURE.

You have to live in Texas (literally, Waco) to be on the show. If it were L.A., you'd spend a year just waiting for permits. And contractors!

I am trying to just get the outside of our house repainted. The exact same color. This should be simple. From Angie's List, I get three estimates. The first guy (a fastidious Asian American with bouffant hair) thought I had a lot more money than I do. He went to his immaculate Prius to pull out an unnecessary binder of satisfied client letters, including one from the Sultan of Botswana(?). Quote: $20,000. The second guy, a white sixtysomething hippie artisan with a back brace, quoted $11,000, but estimated it would take him three and a half months. Until he fell off the ladder and broke his hip—then years could go by.

Third estimate? $3,500. Done in seventy-two hours.

*How is that possible?* I think. *Is the paint radioactive?*

A Latino crew of six shows up on time, 9 a.m. on Tuesday. They're professional, neat, focused. They measure, cover, tape. The next two days, twelve painters show up, working ten-hour shifts. I'm both thrilled and horrified. I'm taking out a calculator trying to figure out how much each guy is getting paid. (Is negative five dollars an hour even possible?)

Ah, well. I have to say, the house looks great.

Just add a throw pillow from Joanna's store that says GUILT.

## A BAD WEEK IN THE KITCHEN

In my home economics class at Malibu Park Junior High in the 1970s, Mrs. Shellkopf taught us girls to:

Punch-hook a rug

Resheath a pillow

Make a recipe box of easy appetizers like "Foxy Franks"—
basically cut-up hot dogs in ketchup, soy sauce, and
brown sugar

Four decades later, I feel a major part of modern home ec training has gone missing. In the history of America, first there were no appliances, then there were helpful appliances, and now we have high-maintenance/too-smart-for-their-own-good appliances.

My house came with a fancy new KitchenAid refrigerator, with monolith-like steel doors that repel magnets—aka: family photos or children's drawings. Arguably, this is an innovation, particularly for ashamed divorced parents. Anyway, the other week, it stops making ice. The fix-it guy from Sears comes over. He says it needs a new part . . . but here's the twist. There's no telling which part because there's no model number on any of Mr. KitchenAid's impassive steel faces.

The only place KitchenAid put the model number was—get ready—on an ink-jet-printed paper sticker glued to the top right inside of the fridge. Right where we keep the milk. So, in fact, our entire household has spent years gradually rubbing off the model number with our forearms while pulling milk in and out of the fridge.

Also, as there's now much busy refilling of ice trays, with the taps twisting on and off, the kitchen faucet starts to leak. I take a wrench—and I'm amazed I can actually find a wrench—to try to tighten the hexagonal spigot . . . nut . . . thingy. Charlie senses I don't know what I'm doing. So he steps in with his manly strength, turns the wrench the wrong way—and with a scream is rocked back with a propulsive roar of water.

I'm embarrassed to say I now hysterically call the Pasadena Fire Department. In thirty seconds, three strong men simply turn off the water line mechanism/joint/rotator under the sink—

Although now of course we had no dishwasher and, weirdly, no microwave because it has been so doused with water its—what do you call it, its brain board—? intelligence board—? smart board—? thinky board has fritzed. We are advised to test the circuit breaker. You mean that thing whose diagram used to be taped to the outside breaker box, which blew away a few years ago in that very strong wind? When all those palm fronds fell (Damoclean swords)?

## LIGHT BULBS

*A Series of Unfortunate Events*

Some light bulbs have burned out in my house, which means that's it for indoor lighting in this house because replacing modern light bulbs is beyond my human ability.

Apparently, it's not enough to match the "flame-tipped candelabra" shapes of burned-out light bulbs, nor to match the sizes of the bases. The lamp warnings (yes, lamp warnings!) say it's crucial not to screw a sixty-watt bulb into a forty-watt socket.

But now I'm standing in the grocery aisle studying a package, thinking, *So much for watts, but what about volts?*

Phone comes out. I google. Here's a wikiHow essay from no less august a source than the *Washington Post*. Its literal title: "How to Navigate the Increasingly Confusing Light Bulb Aisle." It's by David Brooks, proprietor of Just Bulbs in New York. (Just Bulbs? Way back when, *SNL*'s "Scotch Boutique" was an actual parody.)

Brooks addresses a question that has long been—vaguely—haunting me: Why don't our dimmers work with those spirally new CFL (compact fluorescent lamp) bulbs? Apparently, CFLs use so little energy, with their clever phosphor coating, mercury vapor, and argon technology, that "old-model dimmers can't even sense that there is a bulb there to dim."

So in that case, just buy regular bulbs—but instead of wattage you should measure lumens. What are lumens? So easy to remember! Wattage is energy, lumens is brightness. For example, a 100-watt incandescent has about 1,600 lumens, whereas a 40-watt incandescent has about 450 lumens. If you forget, you can check out the handy charts and tables at www.energystar.gov. In your spare time. Feel free, while you're at it, to get a PhD from Cornell in the electromagnetic spectrum.

Further, light bulbs come in a variety of shades. You'll be horrified to learn, as I was, that each color has a temperature rating measured in degrees Kelvin. The lower the Kelvin number, the more yellow the light, the higher the Kelvin, the bluer.

Brooks—who clearly has time on his hands—suggests buying different bulbs with different Kelvin numbers. Why? *To see how you like them.* "Every shade of white is good for a different reason," he says. Modern spaces look better in whiter light, traditional rooms in yellower. A whiter, higher Kelvin light is more popular in the South, a yellower, lower Kelvin light in the North.

In the end, experts recommend not buying too many of any one bulb because, as they say, "the technology is just changing so quickly."

## YANKEE CANDLES

*What Are These?*

We're all familiar with the piney theme candles realtors love for their open houses, like Winter Harvest, Christmas Wreath, Cranberry Potpourri. Or the candles of various girly fruits like Apple, Banana, Papaya.

But the Yankee Candle Store has invented a new 4-D matrix reality where there is a candle scent called Leather. That's right. Leather. Or White Cotton. Do you get it? This is a candle that smells like . . . white cotton. Not yellow cotton. White. What does white cotton smell like? You inhale the candle and suddenly you know! It's surreal!

And that's what you start doing when you take a wrong turn at the mall, like I did the other week. You start methodically unscrewing and snorting these rows and rows of candles like an addict—

Getting a Yankee Candle contact high—

And now you're into the next section—Marguerita Sunset. Caribbean Rum. Luau Colada. This is odd. Why am I standing alone in a mall and snorting candles that smell like hangover-inducing umbrella drinks from a bad Cheech and Chong movie? But were there any *good* Cheech and Chong movies? Who knows?

Next section: food! We are talking candles that smell like, and I quote: "Root Beer. Maple Pancakes. Vanilla Frosting. Fudge Brownie. Bunny Cake."

It's like an Escher painting: Who would burn a candle that *smells* like Bunny Cake while actually *baking* a Bunny Cake? What kind of sugar cleanse would that necessitate? As if in a trance, I buy four. I'm so exhausted from the light bulbs, I can't help it.

## THROWING SOME SHADE

Hannah is complaining about too much light in her bedroom. Her curtains are too gauzy. It makes it hard for her to sleep in 'til noon, which she considers her right on weekends. Because I know nothing, I foolishly say, "Let's get you some blinds!"

Swirling a fresh cup of coffee, I click open Angie's List. I type in "blinds." Do I mean "custom blinds"? Sure! Here's a 10 percent-off coupon—I'm printing money! It's for a highly rated custom blinds guy named Roger. Within two hours he's at my house for a free estimate! #winning!

Roger is charming, friendly, conversational, and—get this! Also a blues musician! He oohs and aahs over my 1906 craftsman house, with its large, beautiful, "unusually sized" windows. Older and wiser now, the phrase "unusually sized" should have been the tip-off that another custom-zero was being custom-added, but I thought nothing of it then. Oh no! Roger was so friendly, I offered him a cup of coffee. Presumably because I was home on a weekday, he asked what I did for a living. I said I was a writer. He asked what kind.

Now I know that this is called emotionally "bonding" and you should not do it when getting a quote unquote "free estimate." In hindsight, I realize I should have said, "I am unemployed," and burst into tears, rather than trying to make my career sound so successful and lucrative. Roger then spends what seems like half an hour—he's thorough!—measuring two windows. And he goes to his truck and returns with a thick, beautifully bound binder. Full of . . . blinds.

Not just blinds. And I quote: "Window treatments of your dreams." And I think, *Who literally dreams of window treatments?*

Someone, because there are honeycomb ones, blackout ones, vertical ones—with different kinds of pulleys, cords, and stylish "valences"—in complicated colors like Banana Ice Milk and Taos Midnight Persimmon. Yankee Candle aromas will be coming next.

Bottom line? For two bedroom windows, it will take three weeks for the custom shades to arrive. Cost? $1,800. "They will look amazing!" Roger enthuses. Inwardly, I agree. They will be the most amazing thing in my teen's messy bedroom piled with laundry, makeup, snarls of electronics, and crumpled tissues. $1,800? We just want something to block light.

After Roger leaves—in an air thick with mutual disappointment—I eye a trifold from Sally's science fair project. I contemplate simply nailing blankets over the windows. In the end, I give Hannah a nice new sleep mask. Although that night I do indeed dream . . . of window treatments.

And Bunny Cake.

## LIBERAL DIRT

For decades, I've never hired a regular cleaning person. Why? Feminist guilt. In *Nickel and Dimed*, journalist Barbara Ehrenreich argued that it's oppressive for a First World woman to pay a Third World sister to scrub her toilets.

So when we first moved into this giant house, I invented a game for my girls and me to play. It was sort of an *Upstairs Downstairs* thing where we pretended to be the servants of wealthy people. I procured "fun" cleaning gear—a Miele vacuum cleaner, battery-powered Swiffer, products like "Kaboom!" Violent and possibly toxic, it cleans your toilet bowl. Sally in particular loved it. "Kaboom!" we yelled, and flushed, like we were getting away with something.

But as girls move into teenhood, they lose the joy and become judgmental. Hannah can be a great refrigerator-cleaner when she puts her mind to it, but she pulls out every gross thing and describes it to me as if it's my fault. It's like an unwanted show-and-tell from a precocious child from some hateful Montessori/Waldorf preschool.

So I finally say, "To hell with Barbara Ehrenreich!" and I hire the cleaning lady Luz our nice gay neighbors enthusiastically recommend, because she needs more clients.

See? By hiring a cleaning professional, I am providing employment in the world. I even insist on paying Luz more than the almost absurdly low price that is quoted.

But then, of course, Luz arrives. She is like an avenging angel sent by Barbara Ehrenreich to haunt me, in my own home.

Truth be told, Luz is on the cusp of being a little too old and frail to be doing this sort of physical labor. In the morning, she'll wheel up a cart with cleaning supplies and enough bottled water to provide hydration for the next, clearly grueling, eight hours.

Luz is mesmerized by this tree in our front yard that, to my surprise—is that what those are?—has guavas. She harvests them so diligently, I worry that, for her, they may represent a major food source.

Also, it pains me to complain, but Luz will rearrange everything. She'll literally move objects randomly from one room to another. It's terrifying. In the evening, I'll reach over to my nightstand, for the important books I was mindfully trying to read, jar of TUMS, reading glasses, *New York Times* crossword—all gone! Why?!?

I feel violated because my intimate things are always being moved—and then I feel reviolated because I'm having such a foot-stomping, First World reaction. Soon I will have to pay more money to take myself to emergency Cleaning Woman Therapy.

## PLEASE DON'T EAT THE BASIL

My new *Green Goddess Cookbook* has an inviting recipe for fresh pesto.

It is a perfect opportunity ("A Passion for Ramps!") for Charlie and me to go to our delightful local farmer's market. Picture charming stands bearing gentle moraines of pesticide-free raspberries, votive candles women from Ventura have insisted on crafting out of honey, and a battered, blue-eyed soul brother crooning Crosby, Stills and Nash. It's less a market than a lifestyle.

We stop at Sunchoke Farm Sisters Produce. It is overflowing with the abundance of the earth: frothy kale, golden beets, gloriously tumbling oyster and shiitake mushrooms. I root around: okay, no, not here, not there . . .

"Do you have basil?" I ask.

"No," the farm lady declares, "too early."

I turn to Charlie. "March is too early for basil?

"I'll just take this parsley then," I say.

"No parsley today," she corrects me. "That's cilantro."

"I could use some dill," Charlie says, pawing through an herb basket of lavender, marjoram, lamb's ear, lemon verbena—"I don't think they have it."

I turn again to Charlie: "So as usual, we have to go to the store."

"Instead of 'farm to table,'" he agrees, "it's 'farm to Von's to table.'"

"Knowing us," I amend, "more likely it will be 'farm to Von's to table, back quickly to Von's, back quickly to table.'"

So we go to Trader Joe's, where they are also out of basil. But they do have live basil plants for $3.99.

"I think that's cool," Charlie says. "Instead of buying dead basil leaves, why not buy a live basil plant, which will continue to make more basil?"

"I'll tell you why," I say. "Remember last year when, charmed by this very concept, I took a basil plant home, placed it as instructed in the half shade and watered it daily? For kind of a long time?"

He doesn't remember—I complained about it so much he blocked it out. I continue: "No new basil leaves ever grew and the plant became rickety and woody and brown, but—the very morning I planned to throw it into the yard clippings bin it burst into flower! Like a ninety-year-old man flinging out giddy 'jazz hands' to fend off a lowering coffin lid. You can't throw away a plant with flowers, so I kept watering it and moving it around and babying it because *one day it might make leaves.* I've been taking care of this basil plant for a year! It puts the pest into pesto!"

We now go to our third stop, Von's, and they too are out of basil. Now truly vexed, losing my passion for ramps, passion for farmers, or passion for passion, I go back to Trader Joe's and buy four potted basil plants. I take them home and, standing on the back porch, I hold each down by the neck and just brutally rip those leaves off. I rip and rip and rip. And then, like Scarlett O'Hara, I scream and hurl the little pots off the side of the deck.

But then I look down at the mutilated tangle of green and think, *What have I done? These were living!—if annoying!—things.*

So I collect the broken plants and apologize to them for murdering them and prop them back up again and now I have five fucking basil plants sunning themselves.

I've accepted it. I am running a small sanatorium—a health spa, really—for lazy basil plants. My house is where basil plants go to retire. Come on over, cilantro!

## TRY NOT TO BE BLINDED BY MY WILDFLOWERS

Charlie and I just want a drought-resistant yard. We meet with a highly recommended Greenfield Heights "master gardener." His estimate includes ten hours of design at $150 an hour and, even then, we will have to *work* with him. There is a lengthy questionnaire about our "aesthetic goals" and "plant preferences." And I'm going, "I already went to college! Just plant something." Where are Chip and Joanna Gaines when you need them? I should just get myself a throw pillow that says YARD.

I try to read online eco-gardening blogs. I fight off a rising sense of inadequacy. Truly mindful eco-gardeners are about more than just drought resistance: it's all about contour maps of bee pollen and rebuilding endangered butterfly habitats by planting native milkweed. Too, I give you: "Viburnifolium is sometimes a bit capricious, so try symphoricarpos?" And Kelvin lumens.

Charlie and I go to nurseries and look at succulents, but we're unable to formulate a plan. Charlie does a Hail Mary pass and buys wildflower seeds. When a gentle rain comes, I put on my Pema Bollywood pants and fling them about with goddess energy. While flinging, I'm hit in the head by one of Luz's guavas. I think that's what it was.

# Stanford Swimming

PHIL ANDREWS IS a lawyer I dated briefly back in grad school (also known as like seven decades—another lifetime—ago).

We didn't have romantic chemistry, but we've always had great friend chemistry. I've joked that I consider Phil my Third Husband. He is very good at adulting.

For instance, let's take a financial meeting I had several years ago at Charles Schwab. Here's what I've written on a notepad from some company called "Bio Water":

"Retirement and write it off and something about medical."

In my mind's eye, a friendly thirtysomething man dressed in charcoal gray business casual (behind a desk and a plant) then says: "Sandra, by all means, you need to form a C corp! *Not* an S corp!" Although, to be honest, I also see a friendly woman, same age, navy blazer (different desk, different plant, facing a different direction) and she's saying: "Sandra, by all means, you need to form an S corp! *Not* a C corp!"

To this day, I don't remember which is right, but I know Phil knows because he sent me all these helpful *Wall Street Journal* arti-cles and walked me through it.

His wife Gita, an extraordinarily beautiful Indian woman from London, is the head of a major philanthropic association. Gita is deeply intelligent and empathetic; she's always e-mailing me thoughtful links of interest on menopause, technology, educating girls.

While Phil and Gita live in Upstate New York, they're in town for the week with their son Liam.

So Charlie, the girls, and I are all going over for dinner. What could go wrong?


GITA'S PARENTS' HOME in Hancock Park looks like a large villa you'd find in Europe, protected by lush non-native hedges.

"Wow—is that a tennis court?" Hannah asks, leaning forward in the Volvo I suddenly wished I'd washed.

"You know what," I admit to my crew. "I forgot that Gita's father is some famous surgeon with a bunch of patents who created the Cedars-Sinai Something Something Center. I guess this is what 'arthroscopic knee surgery' money looks like."

The massive wooden front door swings open, almost like a cas-tle's, and Phil and Gita bound out to greet us. Philip looks like his same absurdly tall six foot three inch self. His temples are gray but his hair looks boyish and full as it always did. Gita's dark glossy hair is in a Catherine Deneuve updo. She moves with the agility of a gym-nast (which I think she once was).

We embrace one another with joyous exclamations.

"It's so wonderful to see you!"

"You guys haven't aged a day!"

"Look how tall and gorgeous the girls are!"

"Charlie! We've heard so much about you!"

"Can we look around?" Hannah asks.

"Of course!" says Gita.

"There's a swing in the back, too," says Phil.

"Phil," Gita teases, "they're not kids." She turns back to the girls, nodding, emphatically. "But yes, absolutely, feel free."

Hannah and Sally take off to explore the grounds. When Charlie turns to admire the house, I notice a band of lining hanging out below his jacket. A stylish guy, he loves to buy designer labels at thrift stores, but sometimes they're not in the most perfect repair.

No matter. No one notices; indeed, it appears that Phil and Charlie have already bonded. Charlie has a friend who lives in Tivoli—the same town Phil and Gita do.

"That's right," Charlie is saying, "Sebastian and I went to Columbia together."

"What a coincidence!" Phil exclaims.

"He loves the town and vibe, but he's always going on about the deer—"

"The deer!" Phil exclaims. "They're pests! They're like vermin—"

"Venison, Sebastian says—"

In the vaulted white kitchen, which calls to mind the apse of a small country church, Gita pulls down wine glasses.

"This is our wonderful Marta," Gita says, introducing us to a smiling sixtyish olive-skinned woman of uncertain ethnicity, in a light blue dress and white apron, stirring various pots. We all nod, bow, trade greetings. Gita leads to the terrazzo-like veranda where a lovely table is set.

"We love this rioja, even though it can be hard to find," Phil says, pouring us wine through an aerator, which makes a faint bubbling sound as it flows.

Charlie takes a sip. "Mmm!" he exclaims, in pleasure. "Rioja, huh? What's the price point on this?" he says, with the confident affability only a WASP can bring.

"It's not expensive," Gita says easily.

"We actually found it on a Zagat list of Great Wines Under $40," Philip says. Charlie and I raise eyebrows amusedly at each other. For us the price cap on a bottle of wine is eight dollars.

Their son Liam appears.

"There he is!" Phil cries out.

"Hello," Liam says politely, shaking our hands, "nice to meet you." Slightly preppy, in collared shirt and maroon sweater, Liam seems to have inherited all of his parents' good DNA. He is handsome and tall, with excellent posture.

"Sorry," Gita says. "He was on the phone with his adviser."

I call the girls in, and we all sit down to dinner.

We exclaim over the salad— "Delicious!" "Almost peppery!" "These tomatoes are from the garden—"

Liam's phone buzzes. He looks at it, looks at his parents, apologetically. "I'm sorry. It's—"

Gita waves her hand. "It's fine." To us: "Sorry. It's kind of a big week." Liam exits.

"So what brings you all to L.A.?" I ask.

"Well, we were making a West Coast swing in any case," Gita says, "so we thought we'd drop in on my parents, before they went to Greece—" She looks at Phil. "Should we tell them? Do you think Liam would mind?"

Phil nods, swallowing wine. "I'm sure it'll be fine." He turns to us, with slight regret, "Liam is in a bit of a quandary."

"A school quandary," Gita adds.

"What sort of school quandary?" Charlie asks.

"Well you know, it's college acceptance season," Phil says.

"Princeton and Yale are really his first choices—because of the great public policy schools—"

"And the classics," Gita says, "and languages—"

"This kid really has an affinity for languages!" Phil says, in a kind of wonder. "He self-taught himself Russian in summer of junior year, when he was interning in Kazakhstan."

"But Liam also got a full scholarship to Stanford," Gita adds, almost sadly, "and of course my father's alma mater is Stanford, so *dadi* is really pushing hard for that."

Liam returns. "Sorry about that."

"But you're interested in Stanford, right?" Gita asks Liam. To us: "Because the swimming is very, very strong."

"Liam was offered a full swim scholarship," Phil adds.

*Swimming*, I think. I'm not even entirely sure my daughters truly *can* swim. In the pool back at their dad's house in Van Nuys, I remember a lot of splashing, wading, dog paddling.

"A Stanford legacy!" Charlie declares heartily. "Well, young sir, what do you think?"

Liam's brow is slightly furrowed. "On the tour, I liked the Chinese Academy, which would help me strengthen my Mandarin . . ."

As Liam continues to describe Stanford, I go into a momentary glaze as I watch, behind him, my daughters chomping on their salads.

Hannah is in her traditional vampire eyeliner, yellow eye shadow, and tank top (due to the heat) with black bra strap showing. With her mocha-hued skin, Hannah looks less like the one-quarter Chinese blend she is than—not to put too fine a point on it—like a straight-up L.A. gang girl. Edging into drag queen.

Sally has all her hair up in a beanie, which anchors her black Elvis Costello glasses. She's so painfully thin she calls to mind Ichabod Crane. She's less eating her salad than worrying it, pushing small exotic creatures around in a tiny pool. I realize she may think that morsel is meat. It is not. It is an oyster mushroom. My eleven-year-old is terrified by this fancy unfamiliar new kind of produce.

"And Palo Alto is an amazing place," finishes Phil.

To which Liam replies, suddenly: "I'm not sure I want to continue swimming." There's a small, tight silence. His parents' eyes widen, but there are no visceral signs of alarm. There is active listening.

"It takes a lot of time. I thought I might want to just focus my hours on crew."

"On the crew of what?" Hannah asks.

"Crew like rowing," I said quickly. "We are rather landlocked here in Los Angeles," I babble, realizing that Los Angeles is the gateway to the Pacific Rim, the ocean falling away below us in sparkling accusation. "I mean Van Nuys."

"Of course, of course," Phil and Gita murmur, as though it is their error.

I'm about to change the subject by asking, "How is Emma enjoying Yale?" But at that instant, in my mind's eye, I see their older daughter Emma, ponytail flashing, as she does a one hundred-meter dash somewhere. Or was it softball? Tennis? Oh no!

Lacrosse. I fear, if mentioned, that my daughters will ask if "lacrosse" is a kind of sparkling water. Not that they're into sparkling water. At Subway, Sally favors a drink where you pour all the different kinds of soda together. It is called a Suicide.

"And what subjects are you interested in, Sally?" Gita asks kindly, the perfect hostess.

"I really like art," Sally says.

"Well, you should come out and visit Bard!" Gita insists. "They have an excellent intersectional arts program!"

"And where are you interested in going to college, Hannah?" Phil asks.

Hannah's quick with an answer I've never heard before. "I want to go to a big school in a big city. Like UCLA."

There's a palpable gust of enthusiasm.

"UCLA is a terrific school!" Philip exclaims. "One of our founding partners is a Bruin."

"There are such excellent public universities in California," Gita adds.

"Absolutely," says Philip. "It's such a boon."

"The UC's have very high Asian populations," Gita says. "Just 12 percent of the state, Asians make up 40 percent of UC students. Some people don't like it," she shakes her head, "what are you going to do?"

"What about Cal?" Phil asks Hannah.

"Berkeley," I clarify.

Hannah replies, "My aunt lives in Northern California. I love it there. But I don't know. The Bay Area is just really really . . ." We all lean in, in curiosity. "Cold."

*I guess in that case* Boston *is out of the question*, I think. (To quote Spinal Tap: "Don't worry. Not much of a college town.")

"How *is* Kaitlin doing?" Phil asks. He turns to Gita. "Sandra's sister is an incredible photographer."

"Well as a matter of fact," I say, almost in disbelief that I have something cool to report, "last summer she had a photo exhibition in Shanghai, and we all went!"

"I really want to go to Shanghai," Liam says. "How was it?"

Brassy Hannah jumps in. "Shanghai? It was crazy!"

What? Where is she going with this?

Uh-oh. Suddenly I know. I pray for her not to continue. Might as well try to contain a natural force.

"With Shanghai driving, traffic laws are viewed as 'suggestions.' You can't step out into a crosswalk if you can see cars coming because, no kidding, they really will not stop." Hannah's hands gesture theatrically. She blazes with the energy of her story. Liam watches her transfixed, perhaps slightly horrified. "We saw a car smash into a motorbike just six feet away, tearing its headlamp off in a splatter of glass and ejecting"—big arm sweep—"the driver, after which, the car just backed up and screeched off!

"And then of course, there were the open air markets," Hannah prompts her sister. I have to admire both her gallantry of helping her shy little sister converse and her stagecraft, while at the same time really regretting the entire tenor of her story.

Sally shakes her head, her eyes welling up.

"What?" Phil asks. "What happened?"

"The open air market in Shanghai is alive," Hannah says, leaping up from the table to describe it, "literally alive. Carp are jumping around your ankles. The floor and walls are wet—it's like being in a car wash. You step over rows of plastic tubs, bubbling with cloudy, lukewarm water swarming with live eels, little water snakes, shrimp with antennas waving!

"And chickens!" she forges on. "Picture, now, a hall of glass-walled rooms. In the first room, laundry baskets explode with freaking-out live chickens. In the second room, the chickens suddenly have their heads off, although they're not completely dead either. Most startling, though, are the big hairy men in sweaty undershirts who are chasing the chickens. Not only are they wrestling the birds down with giant cleavers, they are *doing* so while totally chain-smoking!"

"Oh wow," Liam says. It's hard to know if he is appalled by the story or its teller.

"We saw this guy take a squirming live bullfrog and yank its legs off with pliers!"

Sally makes a whimpering sound. She looks green.

Trying to salvage this tirade with a silky-voiced, tolerance-enhancing Oprah teaching moment, I lean forward and say, "Hannah, in America, it's true, we enjoy so much wonderful food we're spoiled. But in remote parts of China, people are so poor all they have to eat is mice or crickets or—or bullfrogs—or they'll die. It's poverty cuisine."

"But don't you remember what Cousin Zhe said?" Hannah asks. To the others, she adds: "He's Chinese. He said, 'This is what I hate about the Chinese. They insist on having the animal killed in front of them so they can guarantee it's fresh. They need to see the gleam in the animal's eye so they know the merchant's not cheating them.'"

Liam's phone goes off again. "Excuse me."

And in a flash of insight, I see something startling: My children and Philip's are *of a different class.*

With a sudden ice pick in the spine, I realize we haven't heard Cousin Sam report back about any college acceptances. Stanford? In my mind's eye, I see a little village of Legos tumbling. Legos! Good God! What were we thinking?

# "Spring" into Action

## "March" . . . into What?

# Forest Lawn

THIS IS A TALE of two funerals.

Surprisingly, neither is for my dad—!

Let's back up. Here, from my own experience, are the several stages of life of my father.

Middle age (forty through sixty): An eccentric Chinese engineer, Eugene Loh, Sr. is known as "the crazy man of Malibu." He will hitchhike on Pacific Coast Highway, dumpster-dive behind Starbucks, and wear lady's leopard bikini bottoms he found on the beach while doing calisthenics, terrorizing local beachgoers. That is on good days; on bad days he will do his exercises totally naked, balls flying.

"Junior" senior years (sixties and seventies): After my mother's early illness and death, my dad marries a series of three Chinese mail-order brides in order to assure himself care in his old age. That tale became the basis for a solo show I do Off Broadway. So for all his eccentricities, while unpleasant at the time, I am grateful.

Astonishingly, a Malibu grunge rock band named Boy Hits Car records a Pearl Jam–like song about the crazy man of Malibu they actually grew up with. It's called "Mr. Loh." I record a story called

"Mr. Loh's Not Afraid to Be Naked" with both Boy Hits Car and my dad, in studio, for Ira Glass's *This American Life*. Thank you again.

Old age (seventies through eighties): Over this time, a pacemaker is prescribed (and rejected), Parkinson's begins, my dad requests bunion surgery (denied). He moves from his two legs to a walker to a wheelchair—which still doesn't slow him down. Oh no, he'll still wheel himself off to catch the bus to UCLA where, snoring loudly, he will fall asleep in science seminars. While he can no longer do his exercises, he'll still wheel himself down to the beach club to shower, and perhaps flash a few more people.

Extreme old age (nineties): Now my dad moves from teeth to dentures to a GI tube. Due to the exquisite care of his full-time Filipino nurse Thomas, at the rate of $10,000-ish a month, my dad continues to live on and on and on. He's currently ninety-seven. Ninety-seven!

I have to say, after the four-alarm fire that my dad used to be, Thomas keeps our dad very tidy. He's like a neatly typed message in a crisp envelope.

Even with Ensure, there are few calories in, but there are also few calories out. There is much sleeping. When I visit my dad, he's as inactive as he could possibly be. Yet astonishingly, Thomas sends us all group texts with my dad in action poses—in the Jacuzzi, in a birthday hat, pushing a walker with racing stripes.

As Kaitlin says: "It's very *Weekend with Bernie*."


BUT NO. This funeral is for my Uncle Wang, a truly elegant, artistic, and lovable man. He was a painter who used Chinese watercolor techniques to depict American scenery, like the peach-colored, sunset-dappled canyons of Bryce and Zion.

We first visited Shanghai in the 1970s, when I was fifteen, to meet the Chinese—Uncle Wang's—wing of the family. We were shocked by how crowded their quarters were. There were four families on one floor sharing one bathroom. I counted more than twenty toothbrushes, more than twenty small towels strung up above the lone shower like fluttering pennants.

When I visited him next, he and my Aunt Xing had moved to a cramped but still more spacious apartment in New York, way on the Upper West Side, like 123rd Street.

He was doing paintings for restaurants. I remember that he ate his dumplings two-by-two, in even numbers, an Aspergarian Chinese habit I've since myself never gotten over.

His third and final abode was his and Aunt Xing's home in West Covina. It was a yellow ranch-style house with a large-screen television, Wells Fargo wall calendar, and Disney princess toys and such for the grandchildren. On the kitchen counter: Lay's Barbecue Potato Chips, Nilla Wafers, Orange Crush soda.

Uncle Wang and Aunt Xing's journey: more space, fewer people, more Lay's. He made it to ninety-four—good health, joyous manner, gardening one day, had a fall, gone in a week. Not a bad run.


UNCLE WANG'S MEMORIAL begins Tuesday, at Forest Lawn, in West Covina (where I didn't know they had a Forest Lawn), with a viewing of the body.

It's not far from what I expect.

There's mournful organ music. Artificial flowers. A lone Buddhist incense stick (I realize I have absolutely no idea what religion they practice).

I look in the coffin. It's a faintly satanic-looking version of him, to be honest.

While I had decided to spare my tween daughters the viewing, I think the actual burial will be the ritual my overcosseted Western kids can probably handle. But it is I who am thrown for a loop, so unfamiliar am I with the traditions of Forest Lawn. After driving up the customary gently rolling green hills in a convoy, we arrange ourselves in two rows of canvas chairs facing a square predug hole and a box of ashes on a table.

We are joining my cousin Zhe, and his two out-of-town brothers, Zhe's wife, Zhe's engineer son, his son's Latina schoolteacher wife, and their three tumbling Chinese/Latino triplets (we call them either Lachinas or Chitinos).

We are courteously offered Forest Lawn–brand bottled water and Forest Lawn-brand tissues.

We wait.

With an ear-splitting beeping sound, a truck pulls up and two men in Forest Lawn jumpsuits emerge with landscaping tools. As opposed to a speech, the funeral director politely provides us with technical information—how to read the plot numbers, which direction the box will face. He suggests we throw flowers into the hole, which we do. Crying, we take our seats again. We watch as another truck drives up and, for about fifteen minutes, slams the dirt down hard with an incredibly loud hydraulic tamping tool.

It's literally "Bang! Bang! Bang!"

This is followed by a drive to a Chinese seafood restaurant in a mini-mall that—because I make a few wrong turns—turns into a forty-minute drive away.

There's an almost too-gaily colored plastic menu that's all in Chinese, with only blurry color photos of what appear to be pig snouts and earthworms.

Remarkably, Sally is holding it together.

I continue to be haunted by the notion that we are the wrong kind of—possibly downwardly mobile?—Asian.

I say to my daughters: "You know that poem, 'Do not stand at my grave and cry, I am not there, I did not die'? I say when you stand at my grave you'd better cry, a lot, because I put a lot of effort into you two. I want a full hour of crazy grief and then you may go to the Cheesecake Factory." Which we then did.

THE SECOND FUNERAL is for my friend Danielle's dad Calvin. After a bout with cancer, with a bit of Alzheimer's thrown in, Calvin finally died. At eighty-four.

"That's a very humane age," I say, to Andie, Julia, and Marilyn. We're driving to the memorial together. "Eighty-four. That's not young at all, but it's not super old. Given his illnesses, he skipped those extra ten or fifteen years of sheer family money drain."

By contrast to Uncle Wang's memorial, Calvin Cox's memorial is in gorgeous Santa Barbara. The stunning, soaring-beamed church is set among groves on the glorious airy coast, overlooking the sea.

There are lines and lines of cars. God, there must be a thousand people here!

In the entrance hall are lovingly preserved archival photos of Danielle's dad in vibrant life: As a kerchiefed Boy Scout, saluting in his Air Force uniform, in his tuxedo on his wedding day, delirious with his beautiful young 1950s bride.

The service begins with a phalanx of Scots guardsmen, in full regalia, marching in, playing bagpipes. The twinkly white-haired pastor is straight from a Merchant-Ivory movie, with brogue. An opera diva (famous?) movingly sings "Ave Maria," in Latin. Just the right number of friends and family members share stories, both heartwarming and funny. We all laugh and shake our heads in wonderment at such an inspiring life.

Afterward, at the reception, a live pianist plays all of Calvin's favorite music. As we enjoy champagne and themed passed appetizers like Scotch egg and bubble and squeak, magical melodies float over our glade . . .

"You must remember this—a kiss is just a kiss—"

"This is so nice," I whisper to my companions. "What's next? A sunset yacht cruise with dancing? Releasing of balloons, doves, monarch butterflies?"

"By the way," Marilyn asks. "How's your stepmom Helen doing?" My dad's third Chinese wife.

"Oh God," I say, "she was supposed to nurse him into his old age, but instead she was the one who got senile. At seventy-two! My sister had to put her in a home in Fremont where they speak Mandarin. It's costing us $4,000 a month."

"What about her family in China?" Andie asks. "Can't they take care of her?"

"They don't want her back," I say. "Or, if we send her back, they want a fee. I gather either *they're* not that wealthy, or they think *we* are. You know, ugly Americans. With endless cash. We're squished between the First and Third World," I suddenly realize. "It's a very Second World situation."

A bug flies into my champagne flute. I pull it out. We clink glasses. "Hashtag Second World Problems!"

Please join
LYNDA  & STEWART RESNICK
for a cocktail party
in celebration of

ARIANNA HUFFINGTON

and the publication of
her dreamiest book yet

THE SLEEP REVOLUTION

Thursday, April 14
6 p.m. – 8 p.m.

# Sleeping with Arianna Huffington

I T COMES IN the mail. It's beautiful.

Simple, elegant, magic.

It means I get to put off worrying about my children, house, and money for five minutes because . . .

I'm going to a party for Arianna Huffington's new book—*The Sleep Revolution: Transforming Your Life, One Night at a Time*!

It has a great cover. In silvery moonlight, Arianna Huffington sits on an elegant tan divan in a white silky luxurious spa kimono, smiling.

It's like she's inviting us to curl up next to her. Because she's so wonderfully well rested.

I CONFESS I've always secretly admired Arianna Huffington.

Many years ago, in another lifetime, at the *LA Times* Festival of Books, I landed on an incredibly odd humor panel. The panelists were Steve Allen, Arianna Huffington, lefty publisher Paul Krassner, and myself (then "Valley" columnist for the late *Buzz* magazine).

The audience—comprising many older white people in sunbrella hats—was hungry for laughs, but our mismatched panel was not well moderated.

For some important geopolitical reason, Arianna Huffington was keen that afternoon on the subject of Katyusha rockets. The increasingly restive audience began to groan. She shot spiritedly back, in her nasal Greek accent: "I didn't know I was amongst so many Katyusha rocket *supporters*." Louder groan. "Where's the funny!" an elderly man yelled. I think I made a sudden whimsical remark about Arianna and the Katyusha rockets—something which, in my masterful storytelling, I cannot recall. The audience chuckled, temporarily soothed. It was probably at Arianna's expense. It was a nonpremeditated cheeky sophomoric move.

Afterward, my journalist friend Cathy and I slunk into a corner, complaining about how our brilliance in Los Angeles was underappreciated. Suddenly, in a mist of rose-petally perfume (is how I remember it), Arianna appears. Instead of berating me for my snark, her perfectly manicured hand extends us a party invitation on good stationery. She's throwing an elegant soiree that evening for another—much more famous—sulky writer, Christopher Hitchens. (Note: Hitchens had famously written insulting things about Arianna in the past, but she had since breezily forgiven him. Now, because everyone was mad at Hitchens for insulting the Clintons, Arianna is the only person in town who would throw him a party.)

Cathy and I became instant fan girls. We were helpless under Arianna's conquering charm. We rolled over like puppies, offering our bellies to be scratched. Because, to me, it seems, like the Honey Badger? Arianna really doesn't give a shit what anyone thinks of her. And, of course, it was an elegant, warm, perfect party: Arianna's Greek mother hand-rolled baklava, for God's sake!

I felt, in the end, that Arianna Huffington had seen something inside of me that was better than how I saw myself. By her empress-like example, she commanded me to behave better. She bequeathed me more class than I deserved. In short, inside, I have a glowing personal Arianna Huffington, and she is magic.

"I THOUGHT I'D FALLEN off this list, I'm glad to still be on it, or perhaps this is a new list," I'm babbling to Julia, as we troll the racks at Macy's. "The best part? The back of the invite says you can come dressed in either 'business casual' or in pajamas! You can literally come to her *Sleep Revolution* party in your pajamas!"

"Are you sure they really mean that?" Julia asks.

"Yes! The hostess is Lynda Resnick. I googled her. She's the POM Wonderful lady—the woman who invented that magical pomegranate juice! How fun is that? If these gals are putting it out there, I don't want to be the stick-in-the-mud in a navy blazer. Parties are fun, pajamas are fun, and I am fun!" I whirl around to a saleslady. "Where would we find pajamas?"

"But don't you *have* pajamas?" Julia asks, as we ride the escalator.

"I sleep in sweatpants and old T-shirts. If I came in my actual bed-wear, I would look like the help."

"What kind of pajamas are you looking for?"

"I'm picturing, you know, not flowery or boxy pajamas but elegant white silk pajamas reminiscent of Kate Hepburn. In my fantasy, Arianna Huffington welcomes me in *her* white silk pajamas. We clink crystal flutes of prosecco and she says, in her nasal Greek accent, 'To the revolution!'"

Julia wrinkles her nose as she holds up some slacks. "What I really need is a great skirt for this publishing presentation I'm giving. A black A-line skirt. But of course, I've been working so hard, I haven't been exercising and I'm fat. Sheryl Sandberg—how is she so thin? Doesn't she night-eat, with all the Facebook stress? I don't get it. So I went to J. Crew and, indeed, they had the perfect black A-line skirt that forgives all your sins and makes a clean smooth line—"

"Oh great," I say, still thinking about pajamas.

"But only in sizes 0 and 2! The 12s were either white or lime green! I'm not Oprah. I can't pull that off. And then the lining presses against your cellulite. So you have to buy pantyhose with that awful name: 'Cellulite control.'"

"See?" I say. "Pajamas!"

"Ach, I'm so tired of this new women's self-help genre that's all like 'the power female next door,'" Julia grouses on, paging through the racks. "These books come across my desk all the time. An ultra-high-achieving female gives a TEDx Talk. It centers on an 'aha' moment when family and career collide. Typically, New Mom CEO is weeping in a bathroom stall at work, breast milk exploded all over her Tahari suit. Now comes the pivot where the Type AAA female becomes an Everywoman, giving us advice on how to relax. This self-care helps more women to become leaders to further women's rights, which—next turn—deepens our marriages. Really?"

"That seems like a lot," I say.

"Here, look." Julia reads off her phone. "Sheryl Sandberg quote. 'Everyone benefits when men work towards equality. Our relationships and our lives are richer when we lean in together.' What the hell does that even mean? Why must every super-CEO-mom's memoir now be pretzel-twisted into a self-care manifesto?"

"Well, that's the beauty," I say. "We're not LEANING IN. Arianna says TO SLEEP. Resting. It's not complicated. It's human. It's very pure."

With a cry of delight, I pull out the perfect white satiny kimono. Or that's what I think it looks like.

"Wow. This is—?"

Andie, Julia, and I can't get our minds around how big this property is. We've all seen grand houses in Los Angeles, but this is like some Beverly Hills mini-Versailles.

"Lynn and Stuart Resnick own, like, all the water in California," Andie reports, guiding her dusty Honda toward the entrance. It's the only regular car here.

All around us, swinging blonde-haired women of no discernible age at all, like vampires, stick stiletto-heeled shoes out of Maseratis.

Upon entering the soaring, crowded entryway of what looks like a museum, or even a museum storehouse—floor to ceiling, there's so much art, of all different styles and eras—it becomes clear to me that . . .

Out of several hundred guests, not one person is in pajamas—or in anything that suggests pajamas. Unless one sleeps in a skin-tight black possibly snakeskin mini-dress and those six-inch stiletto heels.

It is clear there are no writers or book people we know here. It seems there are only Denizens of The Westside.

The good news is that there's a tower of shrimp on ice, passed canapés, and—I mouth-breathe—"Is that sushi?"

The three of us start eating and drinking madly.

"Here's my question," I say. "If the waiter with the sushi doesn't come up to you, can you go after him? I feel like that sushi guy is actually running away from me."

"No, Sandra," Andie says. "You cannot lumber after waiters like an extra from *The Walking Dead*, knocking over priceless Louis Quatorze art along the way—"

There's a hush of wonder. Clinking of glasses. Ripple of excitement.

Arianna Huffington is here!

Seemingly afloat on the gilded staircase, striking in a red and black evening gown (Balenciaga?), Arianna commands the room thrillingly.

By now, I'm a little glazed from the champagne, but here's the gist of her speech: Americans—stockbrokers! Silicon Valleyites! Uber drivers!—get way less sleep than we should. The Japanese get even less. When traveling the country for her last best seller, *Thrive*, in all the conversations around her, not getting enough sleep was a constant refrain. Everyone was telling Arianna they were getting slammed by work and travel and their devices and sleeping just four hours a night. Arianna herself got a wake-up call when she collapsed in exhaustion and hit her jaw.

She continues, hypnotically, like some Grecian oracle: "Sleep is not downtime. It's a magical portal where you rebuild brain cells, physically repair, connect with your unconscious."

Afterward, amid the teeming throng, I get in line to say hello to Arianna. When I get my brief moment, I throw out my arms and say, "See! I wore pajamas!"

Arianna grasps my hand. "Thank you, darling."

I catch sight of us in a large gilt-framed mirror. She looks like a queen. I look like some sort of puffy-gowned sanatorium patient. I thought it was an elegant kimono. How did this happen?

As we move to the valet station, Julia is excited. "Did you hear that? She said, 'Thank you, darling.'"

"I think you say 'Thank you, darling' when you don't remember someone's name," I say wanly.

WE GO FOR A Groupon nightcap at The Fish Shack near Whitsett and Moorpark. This semigrungy part of the Valley features beat-up-looking white waitresses who look like they haven't slept in eighty years.

Julia narrates aloud from her free *Sleep Revolution* copy: "Rajiv Joshi is managing director of a global non-profit initiative co-founded by Virgin Airlines' Richard Branson. Its mission: 'to help move businesses beyond profit as the only metric of success.' At a meeting in Bellagio, Italy, at just age 31, a severely sleep-deprived Joshi had a seizure. Upon recovery, Joshi shared his newfound philosophy. To wit: 'The struggle for a just and more sustainable world is a marathon, not a sprint. It starts at home with personal sustainability.' "

"Oh my God," I moan, "it's all I can do to remember my changing PIN numbers, much less collapse in Italy while humanizing global businesses with Richard Branson."

"It's this whole new TEDx world," Andie says. "I mean, look at this." She pulls out her phone. "My son Tosh just came back from South by Southwest—"

"Oh cool," Julia says. "I didn't know he was into the Indie music scene."

"He's not," Andie says. "Remember when we were young, back in the 1980s, and we all wanted to be performance artists like Laurie Anderson, writers like Bret Easton Ellis, rockers like—?"

"Flock of Seagulls?" Julia asks. "The Pet Shop Boys?"

"Okay, maybe it wasn't rock's golden age," Andie admits. "By contrast, today what all the cool creative kids want to be are *entrepreneurs*. Look at this." She swipes photos on her phone. "These are from the 'Start Up Village.' It's all the mountain man beards, Modern Primitive earplugs, gals with blue hair. They're inventing fashion apps and microbrews and *crowd-sourced design memes for sustainability*. Tosh said even the food trucks were mix-taping. Picture a twelve-dollar Belgian waffle rolled into a cone filled with kimchi pork and panko-fried chipotle avocado."

"Eww!" Julia and I exclaim, helping ourselves to onion rings that have just arrived, which we are washing down with Bloody Marys.

"First Tosh was excited," Andie continues. "See? Here's his first day's schedule: 'Selling Your Disruptive Startup,' 'Shark, Billionaire, Activist,' 'Outthink the Future with Just 10 Ideas a Day.' In the afternoon: 'The Love Algorithm,' 'Good Is the New Cool,' 'The Future of Emotional Machines.' Check out all these words: 'grocerants,' 'chatbots,' 'artivism,' 'foodporn,' 'wayknowing,' 'biopunk,' 'hackpharma'!

"But by the second day, after several rounds of Red Bull-infused 'accelerator pitches,' Tosh started burning out. Now he starts going to seminars called 'It's Not Ready Yet: The Perfectionist's Struggle,' 'You Can Survive Creative Burnout,' 'The Threat Is Evolving: Are You?' 'Psychopaths in Silicon Valley,' and the 'Entrepreneurs' Guide to Battling Depression and ADHD.' Half of all entrepreneurs have mental health issues and one-third of them suffer from depression.

"Because," Andie finishes triumphantly, "they're not sleeping!"

"Boy, my whole family sleeps like champions," I say, a bit gloomily. "Or at least my daughters do on weekends. They crash out for twelve hours. My second cousin Sabrina is such an accomplished napper her mom calls her 'the palace cat.' Then there's my dad. He naps, ingests Ensure. At ninety-seven, he is personally almost too sustainable."

"The downside of Arianna Huffington's philosophy of sleep is that you can't just sleep," Julia complains. "You have to wake up, refreshed, and produce a TED Talk. I don't know if I even belong in 'the creative class' anymore. Do you see those online 'Master Class' ads? Where Steve Martin teaches comedy and David Mamet teaches playwriting? The other day I found myself clicking on 'Helen Mirren, Acting,' and then thinking, 'What are the odds of my ever finding

myself on a film set, in period costume, Ron Howard yells "Action!"'
and I have to rack my brain, 'What did Helen Mirren say?' "

"I know," I say. "To date, my tooth has been the most viral thing
about me."

Says Andie: "I was sorting old books the other day. Turned one
over. Read the blurb: 'I get courage by reading Virginia Woolf's *A
Writer's Diary*. You must read this diary.' Signed . . . *Sylvia Plath*."

We burst into gales of laughter.

"And why are we all supposed to be tweeting now!" Julia exclaims.
"I just read about a twenty-seven-year-old Silicon Valley billionaire
who mesmerizes his two million followers by tweeting directly to
them seventy-five times a day. Seventy-five! While spinning!"

"Geez!" I say. "I must spend an hour a day just hitting 'unsubscribe' to try to clear my e-mail in-box. Every day the spam comes,
sometimes twenty an hour. It's ridiculous. I'm being pelted with ads
for Viagra, cheap auto insurance, Dr. Oz 'Slim Spray as seen on
*Shark Tank*' alone sends me ten e-mails a day. I get spam in English,
Spanish, and Chinese. That's right. Spam in Chinese. Try to find the
'unsubscribe' button in that hornet's nest."

"And even when there *is* an 'unsubscribe' button in English?"
Andie adds. "Often it's *you* who have to type those wavy letters into
the box to prove *you're* a real person! What—is there some rogue
robotic virus out there maliciously 'unsubscribing' people from their
beloved Viagra ads?"

"The other day," Julia says, "a chatbot literally named 'Girly'—
G-i-r-l-y—was asking me what my high school mascot was. A graduate of Samohi, I typed in, 'Victor Viking'—this dude in a bearskin
and a helmet with horns—and the chatbot politely disagreed. Holy
crap. I just want to pay my gas bill!"

"Sometimes I wonder," I say. "Are there people who hire interns to get rid of their spam so they're free to spin and tweet? And to create the Slim Spray spam ads that constantly come at me? Either you're upriver or downriver, and I need to get out."

We are becoming increasingly Groupon-drunk. "Are these well drinks?" "Why do they call them well drinks?" "I don't think I feel very *well*."

"Even the credit card chip reader?" I say. "It's too much. I'll never get it. I'll never not swipe. It's been too many years. My computer spell-check has become so aggressive. It changes proper names. I type my name in at the end of e-mails—'Best, Sandra'—and it literally changes 'Sandra' to 'Santa.' I can't *see* anything anymore. The new Apple maps are eggshell on white. I step into a spa hotel shower and the shampoo and body wash bottles are labeled in tiny unseeable font. Who showers in their reading glasses?"

"Instead of regularly brewed coffee, we now have to have all those weird little Keurig coffee pods," Julia says. "Why?"

"Just the other morning," I say, "I was listening to Pandora, a nice mellow acoustic Celtic tune. Charmed, I bent down to press 'like' and, I kid you not, THAT'S WHEN THE BAGPIPES STARTED."

"I wonder if a lot of our neurons were used up on older technologies from earlier decades," Andie muses. "Like the diaphragm—remember that little case, and dusting it with corn starch? And the whole frickin' Avent baby bottle system—"

"Oh my God! That Avent baby bottle sterilizer bubble!" Julia exclaims. "That would rotate in the microwave! And then the—the—the *things*," she adds, miming putting bottles into slots.

"And food today!" I say. "What's with this whole 'Build Your Own Burger' mania? Every time I fail. I enthusiastically blue-sky these parts together—feta cheese, banana peppers, onion rings, bacon—and it falls apart and tastes awful!"

"And you're thinking, 'This is why I go to restaurants!'" Andie says. "To pay a chef! To actually 'design' my 'burger'!"

"I'm not that smart," I say. "I don't have an MFA from Cornell in burger design!"

"Last week my daughters wanted to go to Buffalo Wild Wings," Julia says. "Total nightmare. It's lit like a boxing ring. There's a jungle of television screens hanging everywhere showing football. The entire waitstaff is in football jerseys. Buzzers go off, triggering raucous cheers. To distract us, we are handed computer tablets loaded with trivia games. But I can't see very well amid the flashing lights so I mistype my name—instead of 'Julia' I mistakenly type "Jluia.' And then I watch in horror as "Jluia' keeps bombing trivia questions ranging from what running back won the Super Bowl when to what type of cocktail is made with rum—a Bahama Mama.

"The menu brings more bewilderment. It lists things that don't really sound like food—jalapeño poppers, fried pickles, and 'Tailgating Samplers'—which sounds like a cheese curd melted around a car's exhaust pipe—and then finally wings. Traditional or boneless. What? How can wings be boneless?"

"'All right,' I tell our wait-referee. 'We'll get the regular and boneless wing combo.' I realize I may have just ordered 230 wings, but I don't want them to smell fear.

"'Okay,' our wait person says, indicating a giant color wheel. 'Now you need to pick three sauces from here and two dry rubs from here.' Oh no. Chipotle Barbecue. Parmesan Garlic. Hot Thai Honey. Lemongrass Agave. I break into a sweat. Hysterical questions come to mind: How many carbs are in these? What part of a boneless wing is actually chicken? What inning are we in? Are we at first or second down? Help!"

"I'm tired," Andie suddenly says.

"Finally, the magic of Arianna," I say. "A desire for Sleep."

. . .

## Poem

**"CATS UNDERSTAND"**

*by Sally (age eight)*

We take naps in the sun and eat food that's been canned.
When it comes to our lives, cats understand.

# "April" Is the Cruelest Month

# It's Taxing

## The Rube Goldberg Machine, Surprisingly, Breaks Down

C HARLIE IS in crisis.
He has just come back from seeing his tax guy Harold. He is stunned.

BEFORE WE CONTINUE: a word about Charlie and what we might call his Financials. Charlie is a magical sprite who burns prosperity candles, which he buys from his healer Arlestra, for the first forty days of every year. The first time I came home and saw an open flame on the wooden fireplace mantel of my 1906 wooden house, I lost it. "Where is the candle for fire insurance?"

Let's back up further.

Charlie, as I've previously implied, is a downwardly mobile WASP. His grandfather was a CEO of Simmons Mattress—there are memories of swanning around Manhattan in a limo, furs, gold watches. But Charlie's dad was the first apple to fall from the tree, eschewing the family business in favor of printing, insurance . . . barbecuing. Charlie remembers neighborhood parties in Illinois where an entire pig was roasted. So much drinking occurred that when dinner was finally served at 2 a.m., tiki torches had toppled, creating small fires.

Which is to say, third generation after Simmons CEO, Charlie excels at the gentleman's arts: he can really tie a tie, mix a drink, coordinate separates, even for women, and converse on any topic. Indeed, he's so garrulous he'll engage supportively with Jehovah's Witness doorbell-ringers ("because I believe in everything," including prosperity candles).

He can carve a turkey and lay it out on a platter. In fact, there is no food too humble—chicken wings, bratwurst, mini soy dogs—to arrange on a giant platter.

He is also up for dining out every meal of the week, with completely different outfits (different ties, matched with different socks, and different loafers).

In short, Charlie would be a perfect:

University don (perhaps actually named Don)
Walker for an elderly rich lady (which I've encouraged him
    to do, to no avail)
Craftsman house docent (these are the people at historic
    home tours who encourage visitors to "don booties"—
    aka, to encase their shoes in paper footware to protect
    hardwood floors; alternate name suggestion, literally:
    "Don Booties")
Rosearian—it is Pasadena, after all
Affable duke of some small Belgian province

Never mind that there is a garage light that has been clicking on and off for a year. This will continue until 2055. Those are not the gentleman's arts.

Accordingly, Charlie has an ornate system with his Financials. He loves to handwrite checks at our wooden rolltop desk, signing them with a flourish. No e-sig for him. He logs them in a large, impressive leatherette binder. The checks are antique-looking Wells Fargo ones, bearing the images of horse and cart. He enjoys driving those paper checks to the post office in his magical VW.

He stuffs all yellowing paper receipts into various manila envelopes, which bulge in the rolltop, like dough pillows.

Overall, we're fine because rather than *desperately* poor middle-aged bohemians, we're *artisanally* poor. Those are the middle-aged bohemians who somewhere, through the decades, got possession of a house. For my first 1,300-square-foot Van Nuys cottage (bought, sold, parlayed), I have to thank not an amazing movie deal, but the momentary drop in California real estate prices brought on by the 1994 Northridge Earthquake. Thank you, earthquake.

So never mind that, except for my semiregular bouts of college teaching, both of our incomes are sporadic. Our overhead is low.

The mortgage is low, our beater cars are paid off, the insurance is low because the beater cars don't go very fast.

And remember: fine wines for under $8 ($6 is fine, too; even $3.49)!


THE NEXT THING to know is that Charlie and I disagree about our accountants. Mine came thirty years ago via my studio musician ex-husband.

Ben's and my taxes have been complicated since the late 1980s. Example: one day a year, Ben would get in the mail, all at the same time, no fewer than 175 separate checks, ranging from fourteen to thirty-three dollars. These came from sessions Ben would do, once a year, for an eccentric music producer who would fly into L.A. for exactly one week. This guy had made a fortune off of a single ad jingle (for gum?). His dba business name was "Mr. Gone" and his mailing address a P.O. box in Tahiti.

My early tax forms pathetically (you can almost hear the IRS laughing) listed my "profession" as "writer/actor/performance artist/ musician/composer."

I might get as many as twenty-five small 1099s. "College of the Canyons, $800," for an inspiring speech, a $32 check from *This American Life*, which always provided a thrill, if not much actual income, and, for a tiny cameo as a "font professor" I once did on *The Office*, $2.57.

My creative "business" has strange technical needs. Scenery for a Christmas ballet show that has sat in storage in Pico Rivera for ten years. Shipping my mother's ashes to Washington for a theater piece. A small Tantric tapestry for a photo session.

In Los Angeles, some musician's accountants are *themselves* musicians (a blurry web photo may show "Rick the Rock Star Accountant!" in a jet black hair weave and red mustang, holding a toy poodle).

But no. Ben's and my accountants were Jacques, a red-faced fellow in a Hawaiian shirt, and soon after, his new swarthier partner Malik, who looked like a rugged version of Omar Sharif, also in a Hawaiian shirt.

This was who we needed: sympathetic, creative, and perhaps slightly shifty tax guys who would understand one's need to deduct two hundred dollars "for costumes." Also, that musical instruments "depreciate." When one was "self-employed."

Every April, Jacques would wave his hands over my pile of receipts like a douser, and say, "I think you'll owe around $3,000." Fair, as I tend not to pay quarterly taxes.

A couple of years in, Ben and I were sitting on the couch in

Jacques and Malik's ranch-style Valley back house, waiting for Jacques to get some forms. Their home office tended to be pretty messy, with stacks of tax forms everywhere. We look down at the coffee table and see, on the lower deck, slightly but not completely hidden, the *International Male* catalogue and *Euro-Bear* magazine. It is a bonanza of exposed male bubble butts.

It gradually became clear to Ben and me, as the 1990s morphed into the aughts, that our tax accountants were "bears"—large, hirsute gay men into fantasy play and bondage. Jacques and Malik went on mystery vacations to Egypt and Amsterdam. Their tax practice flourished. By the 2010s, they were in a huge mansion on a—I want to say—Southern Glendale hillside among royal palm trees, living like slightly tattered sultans. Looking a little rough by day, it was clear that, by night, this Spanish-style mansion was all about partying, with its kidney-shaped pool, nude white statuary, sackloads of dusty empty wine bottles. There was no female touch, nor apparent maid service. Two large jumpy dogs would greet one, almost but perhaps not quite 100 percent purebred. Think of a garlic butter–colored dog, or a day-old truffle-colored dog. With glittery eyes. Even the dogs may have been partying too hard.

The S&M "cover" became a bit sloppier. Across the hall from Jacques's increasingly disorganized library office, the door was often casually left open to a room featuring a four-poster bed fringed with metal restraints. I saw what appeared to be a clown nose on a stack of 1099s—it was a red rubber ball gag. Mysterious new young men kept joining the practice—brown-skinned, slim-hipped, answering the door in teeny shorty shorts.

Meanwhile, Jacques seemed to be getting a very strange skin condition. That's all I'll say. His teeth were browning and his Hawaiian shirts were becoming tenty. But he never missed a step; he was always in good cheer, and life went on: houseboys made Xeroxes;

wine bottles collected; ball gags mounted; naked statues got a tad more begrimed, but, get this, *taxes were filed.*

"But my guy *gets money back for me*," Charlie would say. "Every year! It's like Christmas in April!"

To which I, the Shanghainese, would say, "That's nothing to be proud of. You shouldn't have paid it in the first place. It means the government has hung on to your money for a year, collecting interest."

Charlie murmurs something about depending on that April "cash flow."

"Honey," I say, "you're a fifty-eight-year-old man and you're still invoking the phrase 'cash flow.'" I don't add that he's driving an almost twenty-year-old VW bug that smells like melted crayons and has 240,000 miles on it, though that certainly is an achievement.

The point being, this year Charlie made just enough to lose his Obamacare health subsidy. I want to say the magic number is somewhere around $42,933. And 57 cents. And a feather. No one saw it coming. Which means instead of getting a refund of $3,500 that he would put into his IRA, to match the $3,000 that would have triggered even more tax savings, he owes $2,200.

He is stunned. It is a crisis.

"It's your tax guy, Harold!" I exclaimed. "Never trust a former child actor!"

"Well, *your* guys are running a dungeon!"

"But it's a very tax-positive dungeon!"

# Physical Update Number 301

## The Flyaway Retina

B Y CONTRAST to Charlie's bronze Obama mystery plan, through my job at a UC, my girls and I have amazing insurance. Sally's vision care alone includes eye exams, dilations, new lenses.

It's almost *too* good.

Because while this gloomy ponytailed hipster is fitting Sally's fancy new frames, he looks up at me.

"What glasses are you wearing?"

"Uh, just some Costco reading glasses," I say, startled. "When I drive, for distance, I just . . . look over the top. I Chuck Schumer-it."

"You need to get an exact prescription," Lemony Snicket says. "You're going to destroy your eyes."

Oh no. Yet another physical ailment.

However, having learned my lesson with the dentist (I now brush and floss re-li-gious-ly), I decide to join Charlie on a trip to Peterson Optical. He has a coupon. Peterson Optical is less a medical establishment than a showcase for designer frames.

"These cat-eye ones are cute," I say—but my browsing is cut off.

A hearty, cheerful Caucasian man in a white lab coat greets Charlie, leading him off to his exam.

A willowy young Asian woman in a green lab coat comes for me. I immediately take my internal "middle-aged monologue" aloud: "I am a nervous patient. It has been so long since I've had an eye exam I don't even understand the new equipment. I may scream or jump out of a window. A lot."

Dr. Sung doesn't say anything. Her expression is opaque.

I have to sit down, look through a lens, and stare at a hot air balloon. Next, I move to another machine and then she does a poof of air that checks for glaucoma. It is a comical test that seems quite unreal to me.

I move anxiously to a chair with a big metal helmet—but this part is actually pleasurable. There's a soothing clicking sound as Dr. Sung dials lenses in and out. There's the pleasure of suddenly seeing clearly and sharply.

That's something I didn't have when young. Everything was clear. Now that we're older, farsightedness is actually a blessing. When I dine out with Charlie, his face is softened, photoshopped, nicely lit. I put on my glasses to scan the menu, look up, and startle. "Whoa, honey! So many pores!"

Not seeing well is also a great Botox deterrent. Instead of worrying about my wrinkles, I just get Target glasses .5 lower than my true prescription.

Dr. Sung does a "follow-the-pen" test, shines a light deep into my eyes. . . . But of course, now she wants to kick it up a notch.

"I can dilate your eye, or you can do an OptiScan. No dilation, they just take a picture. Sound good?"

"Sure!" I say.

But the room she leads me to smells like ammonia.

Now I have to grope this *Aliens Part 2* exoskeleton and press my eye on it. There's a blue flash.

The door blows open. For the first time, Dr. Sung is excited. "Shall we look at your optic nerve?" she asks.

Do I have a choice?

We look. Oh God. The optic nerve looks frightening. It's Frankenstein green, shot through with neon red veins, and has big black spots in the middle. The macula.

"Everything looks fine," she says, "except—what's this?" Click click click.

Dr. Sung studies my optic nerve alertly and intently.

"See this? It looks like a tiny string? It could be part of the normal fabric of the eye, *or it could be a very small tear*. Do you see stars or floaters?"

"No," I insist, immediately seeing both stars and floaters.

I feel defeated. I walked in feeling totally fine. I took an optional test Charlie didn't even take. Now I can worry about a torn-to-ribbons retina.

"Look," I say to Charlie, "in Uganda like in the seventeenth century, what did people do *without* OptiScan? I've never heard of any epidemics of detached retinas."

"Actually my friend Hugh had one. Said it was quite painful."

I complain to Marilyn on the phone: "Come on. It's not like retinas fly off—"

"Oh Barry had that," she says airily, "when we were in Cambria."

"Okay!" I say. "I guess in middle age there *is* an epidemic of detached retinas. Our retinas are just flying off, as we whiz down the 405."

"We were just looking inside Barry's colon," she says tenderly.

"What?"

"Oh yes, Dr. Achebe showed us the movie of his colonoscopy. We thought it would be hideous, but no: Barry's colon looked peaceful, serene, like floating down the Grand Canyon. When are you getting yours? Aren't you overdue?"

"I can't face it right now!"

Although, as Kaitlin says, "After dealing with Papa's and Helen's health and MediCal, my colonoscopy was the high point of my week."

Gah!

# The March for Science

A NDIE IS Facebook-messaging me:

> Are you in? I haven't heard from you!
> What: The March for Science!
> When: Saturday, April 20th, Earth Day!
> Why: Climate Change Awareness!
> Green Energy! Sustainable Living!
> How: (A photo of Andie in a Pussy Hat, pink safety
> goggles, and pink lab coat)

OH JOY, another march, in this brave new era when we're marching all the time. Let me go on record to say I'm totally happy to have done the Women's March a few months earlier. It was quite the novel—and fulfilling—experience.

Yes, in response to that election, initially, we had all been in trauma: the despair, the hysterical Facebook meme-posting, the lying in the bathtub in full black concert dress with a bottle of Costco tequila, listening to all the late-night NPR news shows and wailing.

But ever resourceful, a wildflower growing out of ashes, Andie was the one who spearheaded a positive energy transformation. She printed out patterns, bought wool, and helped us all knit our own pussy hats. (Quite a feat, as I cannot knit, I am farsighted, and am actually visually dyslexic—to me it was like skiing, and my hat only had one real "ear," but no matter!) Andie got us all psyched about the midterm elections. (This was a term we'd never thought about, and the new math was exciting: "In the eleventh and fourteenth districts, if we can just 'flip' them by getting a 59 percent majority in both houses of—")

And now, instead of passively checking the news alerts continually chiming on our iPhones, we were going to hit the streets! We were going to hand-make our own signs! We were going to be marching!

There was such excitement about it, a newness.

Typically we would have grabbed some Starbucks and driven our momwagons over to the march. But according to giddy group text threads lead by Andie, the proper way to get to a march is by this new thing in L.A. called public transportation! In particular, what was it called again? The Metro!

Of course, when my group of four—Hannah, Sally, Charlie, and myself—arrived at the Pasadena "Metro" station, reality began to dawn. Before us was a sea of hundreds of women, in pussy hats, with hand-lettered signs, and plenty of fire, joyously waiting . . . to never, ever get to the march. "Tickets—do we have to buy tickets to ride the Metro?" one woman in a Michelle Obama shirt was excitedly asking. Clearly, few of us had ever taken the Metro. Eventually, slowly, almost apologetically, a train pulled into the station. Compared to the massive crowd it was like a toy Disneyland Dumbo train. It seated— what?—twenty? And we could almost hear it cringe—"Ow"—as six women crammed themselves on.

What sort of medical cannabis were people smoking when they dreamed up this charmingly antiquated scheme? How about canoes? Up the L.A. River? Women unite! Here's your pink wooden paddle thingee!

Realizing that, via the Metro, it would take us 'til Thursday to go twelve miles, the four of us hopped into an insanely surge-priced Uber. Ninety-five dollars later, we joined other jubilant women's marchers, walking shoulder to shoulder, all chanting, drumming, and bearing festive signs as far as the eye could see, the throng so thick you couldn't actually move—

When all at once I remembered I am claustrophobic. I have panic attacks if I sit in the middle seat of an airplane. My mind immediately conjured the movie *Inception*, where the buildings all curve into collapse, and an ensuing sudden stampede, all of our bodies under a pile of pussy hats, with dented wool ears, pink pom-poms rolling.

I informed my household I had to get out of this human mosh pit immediately, and started pushing my way backward through the crowd.

"Are you leaving us, mom?" asked Sally, in disbelief.

Me. The "liberated" mom who was literally abandoning her daughters at a women's march. "Oh, don't worry, honey," I babbled. "You'll be fine. Look at the quality of these fine feminist people. You'll probably find yourself a better mom, maybe one who remembered to bring Trader Joe's snacks or Pirate Booty or bottled water. Enjoy the parade!" I concluded, forgetting that it actually was a march. And we didn't know where it was headed. And we had no car.

Finally finding a bit of daylight on Grand Street, I dropped onto a bus bench and let out a deep breath. Whew! Mind calming. Pulse slowing. At which point, the next menopausal, middle-aged lady crow came to roost. Too much coffee by 10:30 a.m.! Where was the ladies' room? This was like prewar Czechoslovakia!

Across the street, amazingly, was the Hilton Checkers Hotel, letting marchers inside. I wobbled in. On the second floor, an impassable line of pink hats snaked out the ladies' door. Just one guy came out of the mens'. A woman asked, timidly: "Oh, do you mind if we go in?"

"It's a women's march!" a stout woman dressed as a horned uterus (you had to be there) exclaimed. "Of course we should invade the men's restroom!" So we did—but, of course, argh! The two equally middle-aged sisters ahead of me took so long in their stalls they could have been drafting new bipartisan voting legislation.

A full hour later, after being spotty at best, cell phone reception finally popped back on (so many people were taking selfies it had crashed the network). I finally found my group again, under a papiermâché statue of a naked Putin showering with our naked president. By then, I had already mentally made a list of things needed for our next women's march, including Xanax, short-wave radios, and perhaps specially lined pussy hats that could be used as adult diapers. A whole new twist on the saying "Our bodies, ourselves."

ALL OF WHICH is to say now, it's a few months later, the novelty is over, and my world has shifted again. And there is another march on the horizon.

I sigh. Pick up the phone, call Andie.

"You know what?" I say. "As much as I support Earth Day and the Science March and the planet, I don't think I can march."

"What?" she says incredulously.

"I'm incredibly concerned about climate change, but I have some even more immediate life problems here," I say. "Charlie owes money he doesn't have related to Obamacare, which has been its own tortuous road. I've got Hannah calling me crying with some kind of mystery skin ailment. When what she should be crying about is her grades. Sally—"

"We've got to keep the momentum going," Andie says. "We've got to keep showing up. Remember? The midterms are coming. We have to flip both houses—" She goes into the math . . .

My tea dings in the microwave. When I get back on the phone, Andie is continuing . . . "Girls and science— They need female role models— Lego is now making pink blocks— To inspire girls to compete in robotics competitions— Because hands-on STEM learning—"

"Sure, sure," I say to Andie, who, let's be honest, is a graphic designer, not a scientist. "We've all seen that TED Talk about children's creativity by that British guy who was also knighted. We're all enamored of memories of our kids' idyllic elementary schools—the classroom volcanos exploding with baking soda, wonders of milk carton pea plants, sunny farms of ladybugs—"

"It's hands on! Hands on!"

"Well, Sally just did a science fair project that, I'm sorry, was the worst in seventh grade. She literally wrote, 'There's an episode of *Hey Arnold!* where they tried to grow a potato out of a potato—' You understand? All around her, kids are designing robots and water filtration and solar panels and she's trying to grow a potato out of a potato."

"If she's really curious, that's what she should do."

"No, Andie. Science is not just a happy feeling inside. Eventually, inexorably, comes The Ugly. The multiplication tables, long division, algebra, trig, then calculus, if a career in science is really being pursued. Them's the rules, and they're tougher than ever. Take my nephew Sam—4.0 and shut out of every college he applied to— Stanford, UCLA, UC Berkeley, even UC San Diego! Forget the Mentos volcanos and hands-on STEM, I see online that if you have a perfect SAT and a 4.5 GPA, you have a 15 percent chance—that's one five—of getting into UCLA."

"Really?" Andie's truly surprised.

"Turns out, the competition is not just kids who start as early as sixth grade, practicing their PSATs and planning out their high school AP courses. A professor friend of mine at UCLA—she's Asian, so she gets to say it—she says international students from wealthy families in Mainland China are gaming the system! They use fake Beijing High School transcripts, 'gun runners' who take their SATs for them—they morph their ID photos together via computer. They arrive at a UC and don't actually speak English. One student will show up to class with twenty clickers—"

"What are those?"

"These remotes you click to input your answers, via Wi-Fi, when a teacher gives an in-class test. It's for class sizes in the hundreds. So one kid represents twenty, who are at the beach. They literally park their Maseratis in faculty spaces. But they can afford the one hundred dollars a pop for the parking tickets, and the UC makes money, because foreign students pay three times the tuition!"

"Well, as we all know, some wealthy white families do that, too—but at least they don't have to pay three times the tuition. So I guess there's a kind of discrimination even . . . ? Unh . . . hm."

"Although Hannah does tend to do well on standardized tests," I say worriedly. "That could be the saving grace."

We end up agreeing that, while I will stay home with Hannah, who's sick, I will watch Andie and Company's stream on Facebook.

I have to admit, as the morning unfolds, the signs, as usual, are funny.

IF YOU'RE NOT THE SOLUTION, YOU'RE THE PRECIPITATE!
PROTEST COSINE, PROTEST SINE.

WHAT DO WE WANT? EVIDENCE-BASED RESEARCH! WHEN
DO WE WANT IT? AFTER PEER REVIEW!

MITOSIS, NOT DIVISION.

SUPPORT LABS. That was on a dog's back.

And then there were speeches, fewer from scientists than from YouTube science explainers. For me, at least, there were many dubious or perhaps arguable lines that got huge applause:

"Science is inherently political!"

"Science is objective, but it is not neutral!"

And then the New Age chants began: "Science is hope!" "Science is our planet!" "Peace, love, science!"

I heard myself grousing to my daughter: "Sure. It's like 'Nature.' To some, 'Nature' is a beautiful flower. But 'Nature' is also Stage 5 hurricanes and poison frogs that eat their own offspring. And—and pitcher plants."

The chants continue: "Health is science! Safety is science! Clean water is science!"

I yell at the TV: "PS: Nuclear missiles from North Korea? SCIENCE!"

Overall?

I am bad at marches.

I am bad at revolution.

# FlabbraMom

I T'S SALLY's twelfth birthday.

It couldn't come at a worse time. I'm becoming increasingly concerned about her.

At fifteen, Hannah has a million friends—perhaps too many. She's always flouncing around with her motley squad—tripping down the auditorium steps, bent double at one another's jokes, waving my car away. "We're all going to get Boba!"

By contrast, introverted Sally spends a lot of time in her room. Though she's not exactly alone. She's online chatting on "Pesterchum," a teen "fandom" based on the eight-thousand-page online web comic *Homestuck*, while her phone constantly buzzes. She picks it up, types, puts it down. A moment later, it buzzes again. Repeat cycle.

It's just a continually buzzing phone. A little phone pet. "Who are you texting?" I ask.

"Oh," she says, "that's JJ. He was going to commit suicide due to a breakup, went online one last time, found me, I made him laugh! He's wonderful."

. . .

Driving home one afternoon, Sally seems unusually quiet. Worried. "What's wrong?" I ask.

"I can't tell you."

"Tell me."

What spools out is the next level of messy detail. JJ is a fifteen-year-old gay boy in Tampa, Florida, who mostly lives with his aunts. But sometimes he has to go stay at his uncle's, a restaurant manager and an alcoholic who doesn't like gay people. JJ has locked himself in the closet because his uncle is going to hit him.

I am aghast.

"Can he dial 911?"

"No, he says that will make it even worse."

I'm trying to imagine how dialing 911 would make it worse. The police could at least pull you out of the closet—

"What's his uncle's address?"

"I don't know. He won't say."

Completely stumped as to what to do, and upset, I construct a fake badass mom in my mind and I try to impersonate her.

"Sally: you know that if we knew his address and he asked us for help, I WOULD GET ON A PLANE TODAY. I would chopper in and we would get him. But if he doesn't give us any info, we can't."

She seems comforted at the notion that I would chopper in. That seems to staunch the flow, for the moment. The choppering.


The next incident is when I call Sally at her dad's on a Friday night to check in. She seemed monosyllabic and down. Why?

"Because I haven't heard from JJ since last night and I'm afraid."

"Afraid of what?"

"Afraid that he . . ." She can't finish.

With much prompting, she haltingly explains that two weeks earlier, he had slept through the night with a gun next to his bed. The night before, he had said he was depressed and then suddenly ended with "Sorry. Bye. Sorry for everything."

Because I am not a calm person, I'm one step from breathing into a paper bag. That won't help.

What would Badass Mom do?

I think she would say: "I know you're worried but JJ is FINE. Trust me. He's fine." But I don't know that. But just because I don't know, does that mean I shouldn't say it? Is that how parents do things? They project oceanic calm, and things end up fine?

What I end up saying is, "Whatever has happened or not, we have done all we could. We are standing by. And whatever happens, we will be fine."

Again, that seems to sort of work.

An hour later JJ texts her back. His Aunt Jill enrolled him in debate camp this weekend and he didn't have his phone on him. He is fine.

"Camp!" I exult. "You see? How normal! Aunt Jill took him to debate camp!" Sally agrees maybe she overreacted.


I TALK TO my girlfriend Yolanda who, conveniently, is a therapist. I've named her a semigodparent for Sally, mostly so I can get free therapeutic advice.

"Do you think Sally could be depressed?" I ask.

"Well," says Yolanda, "one of the reasons teens get depressed is that they're not getting enough sleep. Girls enter puberty earlier now than ever before. They now enter it as early as seven—"

"What?"

"Well, they don't menstruate for another couple of years, but they're getting that hormone explosion. Their circadian rhythms shift. They really need nine hours of sleep, but often they're getting as few as seven or even four."

"All those devices!"

"Well, look at it this way. Back in the day, we—the parents—used to ride our bikes all afternoon and hang out with our friends on the corner. Our kids can't. The way they shoot the breeze after school is on social media. It's normal."

"Normal! Gah!"

"Just continue trying to gain her trust. Showing that you appreciate who she is. Take an interest in what she loves, what delights her, what interests her."

AND, OF COURSE, more backstory: we're still in recovery from *last* year's birthday debacle.

My daughters' birthdays have always been complicated.

When I was growing up in Southern California in the 1960s and 1970s, all of us kids went to the same schools. The birthday parties were two hours, think: Pin the Tail on the Donkey, Twister, cake.

Fast forward to twenty-first-century Los Angeles.

L.A. public schools today are melting pots. When Hannah went to kindergarten at Valley Alternative in Van Nuys, she was the only blonde in a class of twenty kids. I literally had to train the immigrant families—from Mexico, El Salvador, Armenia, Iran, the Philippines—that birthday parties were something we all could do together.

My way eventually struck my own family as a bit much, being like International Day (with many younger siblings). So after the divorce, when the girls were six and eight, the girls let their dad take over. Utterly sensible, he'd limit the guest list to six, trusting the girls to handle the invites. Big mistake. My girls would invite their friends two days before and, as a result, both reaped birthdays where only one guest came, and they cried.

Although we would try to laugh about it: "Oh, oh, oh—even worse was when just half a child came. Remember? It was just the bottom half, the legs, walking up the porch!"

So last year, Sally's first year in her new middle school, a "gifted" magnet science academy, she wanted to give up childish things.

Sally had a vision. She described it with excitement.

"Friday night, six to ten, coed sleepover. We'll have a cookie-decorating contest, a baby food-tasting contest, and a marshmallow-eating contest called Chubby Monkey I saw on YouTube!"

She has been talking it up with other giddy sixth graders.

Small wrinkle: none of their parents know, because five days before, no actual invite has been handed out.

So here's where I kick into gear.

Helicopter parents? Amateurs! Me—I'm less helicopter mom than Robert Duvall in *Apocalypse Now*. Think fleet of choppers, napalm, Ride of the Valkyries.

True: I can't even *conceive* of a parent who would drive his kid from Sherman Oaks, where Sally's school is, to Pasadena, where my house is, on a Friday night, wait for four hours, then pick the kid up. It's like hoping for a unicorn, which is probably another thing on Sally's wish list.

As this is a new school, I know none of these kids or their parents. But I do have the homework group e-mail list. Gingerly I pull it up. It is an alphabet soup of parental first names like JohnM and Nancy123 and then more helpful addresses like FloresFamily—or they would be helpful if Sally knew any last names.

So, wincing at the possible illegality, I send out a few tentative, apologetic notes that say, "My eleven-year-old guesses you are the parent of her friend Dan. She would like to invite him to her birthday party Friday night in a venue very, very far from you. I am not a serial killer. If this is not Dan's dad, please ignore."

And the first note bounces back immediately from a mom who says, indeed, we have the wrong family. And I realize I have inadvertently informed a parent that my daughter Sally is having a party and her son is not invited. Terrific!

But then a turn happens.

A dad writes, amazingly, that his daughter wants to attend the party, so the parents will drop her off at six, go to dinner, and pick her up at ten. It'll be date night!

Another mom writes that her son would love to come but as she's already madly chauffeuring her three other children that night, can I give him a ride?

We're up to fourteen RSVPs, which is four more kids than I really want, for an "optional sleepover" party—but I figure there will be attrition.

The first sign of trouble is after school, when I'm picking up the children. I won't say how many children will officially fit in my car, but I can say I wish there had been two less children. That said, it was surprising how automatically they folded themselves on the floor into sardine can position, as though this was a drill done many times.

By the time I gingerly make it back home via side streets, it is four o'clock, and everyone is *starving*. The pizzas are supposed to arrive when the party starts at six and so, as if in a dream, I get out the skillet and start making quesadillas. We now have seven tweens running around our backyard and it is three too many. Those creatures are big—by that I mean the girls, not the boys, who are four feet tall and punching one another.

More kids are arriving, including several who not only did not RSVP—"Glen? Hi, Glen! Who's Glen?"—to this day, I'm not sure they were even at the right address. I had prepared a Yankee Swap present game for 14 kids, now I have 20. There were 14 reasonably good gifts—now I'm frantically throwing stuff into gift bags: stale Halloween candy, a kitchen sponge, an old tennis ball, trying to ignore the fact that they are technically wine bags.

"I saw Slender Man!" some young punk yells. Now a dozen children run out of the gate and down the street, with me running after them, yelling, "I'm texting your parents!" Back-sasses an angel-faced blonde, "What they don't know won't hurt them!"

I'm half-tempted to hit them over the head with a shovel.

All around Sally are sixth graders inhaling helium and shrieking the Spice Girls' "Tell me what you want, what you really really want!"

"Oh my God," she wails, "this is the worst birthday ever!"


BUT HERE COMES surprising good news.

Sally has a plan for her twelfth birthday. She describes it to me while sitting at her desk, and carving troll horns out of balsa wood.

Sally wants to attend the Anime Convention in Long Beach. A gaggle of online *Homestuck* "cosplay" friends are coming. If I will drive her, she will be so grateful. No gifts necessary.

I am delighted this is so simple.

That same weekend, Ben will drive Hannah to her first practice SAT. "We're *on* it," the father of my children declares.

So my focus can be only Sally and *on her interests!*

Si, si puede!

I am going to educate myself on this. To get closer!

I eagerly don my Costco reading glasses and peruse the Anime

Convention website. What fascinating workshops and panels are they offering? Sample titles:

My Hamachi Designs: Harajuku Dog Fashion
Foam Prop Making with Shawshank
DokiDoki Chu!: Sound in Anime
Osomatsu-san Fan Panel ("So you're finally here, Karamatsu Girls!")
Wigs 101 and Wig Repair
Hot Glue Cosplay with Snugzmeow
Learn to Yoyo
Stunt-Fighting

Closer to my expertise, there are multiple Pokémon GO workshops. I am a secret middle-aged Pokémon GO addict. My girls introduced me to it, then went back to school and got bored with it. I stayed on. In case Sally and I get separated, I will have a backup activity.

In printing out our tickets, they ask me to choose my "cosplay name." I pick "FlabbraMom." Logic? Sally's Pokémon GO name is "Flabbra," and I am her mother.

What could go wrong?

THE MORNING OF, Sally is dressed as "Dave Strider" from *Homestuck* (cropped blonde wig, aviator sunglasses, homemade sword).

I am dressed as Her Mother, in T-shirt, khaki pants, and New Balance tennies. Thinking ahead to the long day, I have packed a soft cooler of Costco salami and cheese. #Winning!

Whizzing south on the Long Beach Freeway, I pelt Sally with questions. "So in *Homestuck*, there is a 'living' world and a 'dead' world, right?"

"Well, there are several different planets—"

"Where the trolls live, right? Not elves."

"Correct. There's Terezi—"

"Terezi!" I exclaim, moving aside the neurons responsible for correctly spelling Saoirse Ronan (recent several-times-appearing *NY Times* crossword clue). "Terezi is blue. She has the Aquarius sign. She's from the underworld?"

I think we've done well enough with that conversation that we now deserve a respite. After mooring the Volvo in the cavernous parking structure, we now join several hundred people in a line that snakes around the convention center. Above us, blue pennants flutter under the sun. Beyond us, the harbor sparkles.

The anime conventioneers make up a colorful group. Costume genres include Japanese anime—Asian girls with high neon pink or green pigtails—Harajuku dogs? In quasi–French maid dresses, silver disco boots, angel wings.

Alice in Wonderlanders—that's girls *and* boys, often in cross-gender outfits. For example, there goes a male Alice. Rollerblading. Six feet tall. Full black beard. And pigtails.

There are assorted zombies, steam punkers, Power Rangers, Greek underworld demons, a vague category I might refer to as "Dead Renaissance Fairies," and what appear to be floppy-eared Never-Ending Story dogs, with fluffy glitter tails ("furries"?).

It is fun to stand in this line and people-watch . . . for the first fifteen, twenty minutes. But then, with the intensifying heat of the sun reflecting on various battle weapons around me, my left ("flyaway") retina is starting to pulse. I'm starting to see stars and floaters. I cup my eye in my hand.

In front of me is an orange Manga Man in full body suit with a trident. I lean forward, give a light tap.

"Excuse me," I say. "Does it feel to you like this line is not actually moving?" Manga Man barely nods—although his stiffness may be due to his costume. "What's the deal? Anyone know what the deal is?" I call out cheerfully, to my line mates. Various masked and feathered heads shake. No clue. No urgency, either.

Anime land's gentle denizens seem to already have plenty to do with twirling and surreptitiously repairing (with duct tape) their elaborate props.

"Man, if I were to invade a country, cosplayers are the last people I would take!" I joke a bit too loudly to Sally, who looks stonily forward.

Five minutes later something snaps. "I've had it," I say sharply to Sally.

Her eyes widen. "No, mom. Please."

Tell it to the hand.

A mom on the go, I stride in my New Balance tennies past several hundred conventioneers to the front entrance. There I accost the laconic Anime Convention guy in a man bun and wrinkled yellow security vest.

"How long will this take?" I babble wildly. "What's going on? We've driven five, three, seventeen hours!"

Man Bun mumbles something about some printer being broken, so they're kinda behind on printing badges.

"I know this is not your fault," I say, "but we've been waiting over an hour and my daughter and I have a critical panel at eleven." (I moved the time up two hours.) "I want to speak to your supervisor!"

In confusion, Man Bun waves over a similarly young and clueless guy. He at least is wearing a blue Long Beach Convention Center blazer and has on his "customer service" face. He listens attentively, then produces a surprising response: "Oh, you're with Indie. Indie films. Sundance. That another entrance."

I have no idea what he's talking about—then I realize he's seeing the Sundance (Theater Lab) logo on my T-shirt. Half my face wants to go, "That's right. Maybe I am. In Indie films. With Sundance."

But now we're joined by a no-nonsense chunky anime dominatrix in black leather, with blonde braids crossed over the top of her head. In more than one way, I sense she is "the heavy."

"Excuse me," she snaps, "is there some sort of *problem* here?"

With a big whoosh of hot flash, I push past Man Bun, Customer Service, and Dominatrix Girl and shriek: "Let me see your head producers! Right now! I'm from the press!"

There's momentary confusion among the yellow-vested staffers as I blow past them into the (pleasantly air-conditioned) convention center lobby— As though I have any idea where I am going— Are they going to chase me? What of it?

To forestall being physically thrown out of the convention center, I whip out my iPhone and say into it, very very quickly and very, very tersely, like a very, very important *Anime Magazine* editor furious because her top-priority credentials are not in order: "Yes. No. Of course! New York is on it. The New York office!"

For good measure, I throw in some fancy SXSW language. "Artivism!" "Hackpharma!" "Grocerants!"

Speeding away from my potential captors, I see to my left, through walls of glass, the still-unmoving line of fairypeople, wilting in the Long Beach sun. There are double doors every fifteen feet. I realize, like some anime Norma Rae liberator, I can just push open door after door and let everyone in.

Barring that, I could just let Sally in—

And there she is, behind orange Manga Man. I text her: "Honey, look to your left."

I see her look down at her phone, then around in confusion.

I tap on the glass. Tap, tap, tap. Wave. Everyone sees me but my daughter. Some guy dressed as a starfish pokes her on the shoulder and gestures toward me with one of his five golden foam points. Sally sees me and starts in terror.

You have to understand that Sally is a tiny police girl. One of her major pet peeves is jaywalking. When I'm driving, she wants both hands firmly on the steering wheel at all times, even at stoplights. "'Two and ten o'clock, mom! Two and ten."

No matter.

I shove open the doors and attempt to pull her in, with some difficulty. "Come in. Quickly."

"What are we doing, mom?" she wails, her skinny shoulders shaking in horror. I'm now firmly yanking a half-panicked child down the convention hall to . . . I don't know where.

"Will we get in trouble?" Sally pleads. "I think we should go back and wait outside!"

Seeing that we're attracting stares, I put my phone up to my ear again. "Yes, yes, the talent is here," I say curtly. "No, we didn't. I made that call. The L.A. office is on it."

"I can see your home screen," she asks. "Are you actually on the phone?"

I whirl toward her. "What do YOU think, Brad? What do you and the committee really think? Whether or not I am, or if, in fact, we are?"

"MOM?" Sally cries out, grasping my arm. "WHY ARE YOU PRETENDING TO TALK ON YOUR CELL PHONE?"

I pull us into an alcove. "Excuse me for just a moment—quick L.A. conference," I say tersely, hanging up the fake phone.

"Why is this fair?" Sally asks. "Why should we break out of the line when everyone outside has to wait? How are we special?"

It's, really, the very opposite of an after-school special.

"Let me tell *you* what's not fair," I say, waggling a finger. "Some kid out there drove three hours to get here, he spent sixty dollars, maybe he only has five hours to spend here, and three hours of that he's going to spend standing in line! How is *that* fair?" I finish, triumphantly. "It's sheer capitalism!"

Sally crumples in the corner, her sword collapsed beside her.

And then I see it. The Press Booth. Two bored young women. No one in line. I fumble through my fanny pack, whip out an expired NPR badge, and stride toward the bench.

"I'm with NPR—press!" I declare.

"Press," one says, picking up another clipboard. "I don't see—?"

"No no, we're not on *that* list, we paid—" Everything I am saying is contradictory, but I'm impatient, curt, distracted by my phone. "Yes, Brad. It's not here. New York is unaware. Ravi Joseph is on it—yep, the sleep thing, Arianna Huffington's guy." Riled to the max, I put my hand over my iPhone, and unveil my ultimate action hero weapon—my Menopause Face.

"WE JUST NEED OUR @#!@#!@# BADGES!!!"

In wide-eyed terror, the girls assemble our badges and peel and paste PRESS stickers to them, handing them over.

Mine importantly reads: "PRESS." Official NPR byline: "FLABBRAMOM."

And I can see, just beyond, magically, the line is now moving. Orange Manga Man and Starfish are being warmly welcomed into the front door. In this whole hostile lying cheating gambit, not only did I not save us time, my daughter thinks I'm an asshole.

SALLY IMMEDIATELY FINDS her fellow Homestuckers and, with palpable relief, disappears. So here Manhattan publishing's very own "FlabbraMom" stands alone in her New Balances. With a purselike soft cooler of sweaty Costco salami.

Ahead of me is the Pokémon GO panel. I brighten. Enter the room. My people!

Okay, I don't know what I thought other Pokémon GO players would look like. I guess I expected them to be like me, sort of intelligent and obsessive and on the spectrum, sure, and yet, somehow, wry. Or, at the very least, in the good sweatpants.

Are you addicted to Candy Crush? Online Boggle? Tetris? Do you ever wonder what other Tetris players look like?

If you do, please consider the Oscar Wilde quote: "The brotherhood of man is not a mere poet's dream; it is a most depressing and humiliating reality."

This was the Scared Straight of Middle-Aged Pokémon GO Players.

People here are old, young, thin, obese. The room is a sea of yellow Pikachu hats, Squirtle earmuffs, Pokémon stuffed animals hanging off Pokémon backpacks. One fortysomething guy in a blue Mystic (that's my team) Bunny costume, with leotards and mask, is playing Pokémon GO the whole time, swiping away with his blue-gloved paw.

I need some air.

I leave the convention center and walk down to Long Beach's lagoon, its sunny perimeter festooned with shops and restaurants. The boardwalk teems with hundreds of people . . . of which literally nine out of ten are swiping vigorously on their phones.

"A Lapras!" someone exclaims. "Where?" "There!" Three hundred people veer left like a fleet of birds.

A Lapras? In spite of myself, I open my Pokémon GO. Lapras are very rare! A sightseeing boat cruises into the lagoon. From the top deck, a white-uniformed captain shouts over the megaphone: "Dragonite! By the lighthouse! Dragonite!" With a cry of excitement, the entire mob charges up the hill . . . and then everyone stands around, looking down at their phones, as though standing around a giant beached whale.

And then I realize: the fishing boat captain was joking with us!

Never mind that a more successful parent would be driving her child to Kumon, a tristate robotics meet, or a fencing competition— something to enhance the college résumé! This is a whole new low.

Hungry, I sit on a rock and eat the disgusting salami. My iPhone jumps with a text from Hannah:

**Mom, please pick up. I'm so scared and sad. They wouldn't let me take the SAT this morning because I FORGOT MY ID. I thought I had it. It was in my denim bag. I've been just crying and crying and crying. ;(**

# "May" I Have a Couple of Ambien?

# C-Plus Tiger Mom

A RGH!
Thus far, I've resisted being a Tiger Mom.

I can't face the pressure of parenting really gifted children. Every time I watch the Olympics, I feel for the parents watching their gymnast daughters do the vault. The last time Michael Phelps swam, I was too nervous to watch—due to the narrative now that Phelps was "the oldest" in the pool at thirty-one. I was so anxious for him.

At the same time, I was thinking, *He has twenty-three medals already! Who cares?*

BUT NOW IT'S A different time. High noon.

My parenting is terrible. In my goddess pants, I have let everything drift. I'm on the phone with Tiger Aunt Kaitlin, complaining.

"Before grades actually counted, Hannah used to get easy straight As and now I'm seeing all kinds of letters, some I don't even recognize. Is an 'epsilon' a grade? What does it mean that her AP biology grade is a 'negative epsilon'? Why, next to AP history, is there an emoji of a little paper hat and a McDonald's logo?"

"You may be overreacting," Tiger Aunt K says, unconvincingly, because if there's anyone who overreacts, it's her.

"I'm not!" I say. "At UC Irvine, where I teach, a 'second-tier' UC, the average GPA is a 3.9. I think Hannah's lucky right now to be holding a 3.6. At this point, *any* UC would be amazing. Forget Berkeley or UCLA. UC Davis would be incredible, as would UC Santa Cruz, UC Riverside, UC Merced—" I wonder aloud: "Is there a UC below Merced?"

"Stop worrying!" Charlie says. "Your sister Kaitlin went to UCLA. That means Hannah will be a shoo-in. She's a 'legacy'!"

I snap at him: " 'Legacy' means your dad donated $20 million to the cancer center, not that you were a Moderately Gifted Child in 1979."

TROLLING THE INTERNET, I find a book: *Start Late, Finish Rich*. It's for losers—I mean "people over fifty with no retirement savings." The book is optimistic. It's forgiving. You can "start late!"

I love this Pema Chödrön spirit. As a corollary, while thus far, I've been a lazy Panda Mom, maybe I still have time to get my daughters on track to go to college. Somewhere.

First item of business? Hannah. Taking up any kind of sport to enhance her college résumé, even an obscure and possibly less-than-competitive one like the luge ("Start late!") is out of the question. Athletic activity is inimical to Hannah. I remember in second grade, when I took her to a free tennis lesson. There a merry line of children bobbed, exuberantly hitting yellow balls—pop, pop, pop—into the blue! Yonder, under a tree, my daughter lay, making artistic piles of leaves because "the sun makes her eyes hurt." So #palacecat.

However, scared straight from forgetting her ID, Hannah has agreed to do an online SAT course with a company called Prep-Scholar, created by actual Harvard graduate Allen Cheng. Otherwise known as My Fourth Husband, Allen Cheng has complete faith in Hannah, and in everyone else who has paid four hundred dollars, sending us both constant cheerful e-mails applauding her progress at completing modules.

Then there is Sally. Her problem has long been . . . I'd like to say, perfectionism? But it's really more like procrastination.

Example: in fifth grade, for her big "state" project? Sally got assigned Hawaii. We were all stunned. No one in two generations of our family had ever gotten a cool state. In our own childhoods, my sister, brother, and I had all gotten normal, boring states like Michigan, Rhode Island, Virginia. My sister thought Virginia was special because of all the presidents—that's how little we had to work with.

Although she had a full twelve weeks, Sally jumped boldly out of the gate, brainstorming the exploding Mentos volcano, hula dancers, and a motorized shark leaping out of a game board!

When you are divorced, and the children go back and forth, you naturally assume schoolwork is being done at the other parent's house. But no, Sunday morning before it's due, Sally comes into my bedroom and says, coyly, "I'd like to invite you to be part of my motivation army." She has done nothing.

At the eleventh hour, we slam together not a brilliant project. The centerpiece was a pencil drawing of the Hawaiian state bird. It is called "the nene."

Meanwhile, I noticed, around the same time, our dad's Filipino caregiver, Thomas, father of four children, was actually building, in the garage, his own fifth-grade son's state project. New York. It was a large box featuring a full-on replica of the Statue of Liberty, holding her torch out over a harbor of actual water, which was slowly being patrolled by an actual motorized boat. Hardworking immigrants win it again.

First World question: Should I stay out of this? Let the chips fall where they may? Use this as a teaching moment to learn responsibility and consequences?

UPON SORTING PAPERS, I come across this report (from which grade? No clue).

### OWLS
*by Sally (age ten)*

Some things that I know about owls are that they have large eyes, a large head, and that they are carnivores. Owls come in all different colors, shapes, sizes and they all have a different name. For example the Barn owl, the Elf owl, the Great Horned owl, and the Snowy owl, they all come from the same family, THE OWLS! Okay, that is pretty much all I know about OWLS.

OKAY, SO THE UPSIDE is that Sally has this narrow band of ability where she scores like a Korean on standardized math tests. This has landed her in the rigorous "gifted" LAUSD science academy of the bad Slenderman party. It is full of other bright and lazy children who also watch anime until 3 a.m. and have terrible study habits.

Gluing this ecosystem together are us parents, both bloated with vanity about our superkids and baffled as to why they're bringing home Ds and Fs. To explain why, the teachers now send home a take-home biology test that "parents and children can work on together." Why? Because apparently, as parents of teens, our blood pressure is too low. But newly Tiger Mom-ing it (paging Amy Chua! Ding, ding, ding!), I embrace the opportunity. After all, I am half Asian, a (okay, adjunct) professor of science communication, and, before I failed my own Shanghainese Tiger Father and switched to the liberal arts (which, as I like to say, "to a Chinese father is like pole dancing"), I actually earned a degree in physics from Caltech. I even drive over to my alma mater to check out a copy of the actual Campbell biology text the class is using! Booyah, suckahs!

Very well! Question one! Pencils out!

"The structural integrity of bacteria is to peptidoglycan as the structural integrity of plant spores is to lignin, cellulose, secondary compounds or sporopollenin."

That's question one out of seventy-six.

No problem. I will dive in, become one with sporopollenin.

I yellow highlight away, feeding Sally healthful snacks to keep her awake. We are eating pita chips in hummus like Grand Uncle Wang would, two-by-two.

Sally slumps against her stuffed animals, reading in her weird anime cartoon voice:

"Diatoms are encased in Petri-platelike cases (valves) made of translucent hydrated silica whose thickness can be varied. At certain times, diatoms store excess calories in the form of the liquid polysaccharide, laminarin, and at other times as oil."

I answer in a cartoon voice. Also, of course, we argue about stuff neither of us really understands.

"Maybe if the messenger RNA dudes are all up in the cytosol, maybe they don't NEED ATP? Because of the hydrogen gradient? In the binary fission S-phase?"

Never mind that we spend fifteen hours of our weekend on this. It's worth it! By Sunday night, we have seventy-six answers we feel really great about.

Until our score comes back. Seventy-nine percent.

WTF!? I'm a C-plus Tiger Mom.


BUT NEXT WEEK, because we end up studying the wrong chapter, it's even worse. On her Monday quiz, Sally gets an F.

With her semiphotographic memory, though, Sally is able to recall all 32 questions. So she cheers herself up by giving me the test, and I also get an F. Although at 16 out of 32, I consider it a fairly high F.

"We are winning," I say sagely. "If very, very slowly."


USING FLORAL FOAM, pipe cleaners, and, literally, buttons from Michael's, I make Sally a model of the cell that looks less like the cell in the book than some kind of woolly exploding craft virus.

My friend Wendy, a lawyer, commiserates: "When Noah was in school, my husband and I couldn't win either way. You know what Chet and I got on our Navajo village? A D-plus. That smarts when you're forty-seven. Noah was having trouble on a big eighth-grade essay, so I rewrote it and gave it a snappy new title: 'Strawberry Fields Forever: The Plight of the Migrant Worker in the Central Valley.' "

"So clever!" I erupt.

"Yes," Wendy agrees. "The 'Beatles colon' title thing is a construction Chet invented in college, with his infamous 'It's Been a Hard Day's Night: Prostitution in Turn-of-the-Century Chicago.' But 'Strawberry Fields' backfired. To his horror, Noah won a trophy for the essay I wrote at his middle school assembly. He cried all the way home."

Sure, but Noah is currently attending Northwestern. *Strawberry Fields Forever indeed!* In fact, I see a way in. Like Wendy, I can stick to my strengths.

This weekend, Sally's homework includes rereading the *Story of Islam*, reviewing the hydrophilic system, and also, "Write eight poems for the eight parts of speech." In rhyming couplets.

This strikes Sally as impossible.

Lying on her bed, capsized under a Sponge Bob pillow, she declares: "I'm not even going to try."

"Honey, if you don't even try, you'll get an F!"

"Fine!"

"I can help you, honey! Maybe you and mommy can write them together!"

"Hashtag Living Nightmare."

So I write them myself and I think they came out rather well! Of course, I've had no sleep because I worked on them for fourteen hours and at one point fell into a trance where Dr. Seuss's Cat in the Hat was coming after me with a bowling shoe. My humble hope, however, is that they will become minor classics, or at least will earn a higher grade than the C we just got in biology.

I give you:

### PARTS OF SPEECH Poems

*by Sandra (age fifty-six)*

**VERB** (a spinster English teacher, way too excited about grammar!)

*Is there a noun you might disturb?*
*Pair it with an action VERB!*
*Nouns just sit there fat and slow*
*They have nowhere else to go*
*Nouns wait still like birds on wire*
*Don't blame them, they're just plain tired*
*But here come verbs like gusts of wind*
*These fat noun birds?*

*No longer pinned!*
*Running, jumping, skipping, hopping*
*Verbs make nouns start rising, dropping*
*When it's done, after all that flap*
*Verbs will let you SLEEP and NAP.*

**NOUN** (a Mafia teamster taking an English class in prison)

*Who is Bud or Beth or Bea?*
*"What strange mortals we all be!"*
*Dogs and cats and mules and goats*
*Planes and trains and ships and boats*
*Cakes and toast and steak and soup*
*Dirt and sand and pee and poop*
*Some are mighty, some are small*
*Some like air aren't there at all*
*NOUNS are things that own and do*
*They're parts of speech like me and you*
*Makes no difference which you like*
*We are NOUNS so take a hike!*

**ADJECTIVE** (a C student trying for a B, can't close the deal)

*Sunny, oily, round, and curled*
*ADJECTIVES describe our world*
*Without them we'd just have a name*
*And look and sound and smell the same*
*An adjective can help a meal*
*Transform itself from drab to veal—*
*Oh no, not veal, but veal that's tasty*
*Dang, that rhyme was much too hasty*

*That former rhyme, that sloppy rhyme*
*That sapped pure wit and precious time*
*This sleepy day, when dull thoughts roam*
*Makes a middling effort, shaky poem.*


**ADVERB** (*Devil Wears Prada*, a snobby—maybe female—film exec)

*To make a film of Jack and Jill*
*Requires more than one brown hill*
*The hill you need, but it's not thrilling*
*Noun on film won't make a killing*
*The kids went up, but slowly, quickly?*
*Jill went gaily, Jack went slickly?*
*Is that the reason Jack fell down?*
*He ran too fast, and broke his crown?*
*ADVERBS tell us how they acted*
*How they tumbled, hill impacted*
*Movement coaching, voice inflection*
*Cast two kids who take direction.*


**PRONOUN** (salty ninety-four-year-old country grandma)

*He and she and we and me*
*Are simpler names for folks we see*
*Like at Thanksgiving, round the table*
*Baby Frederick? Grandpa Mabel?*
*Uncle Todd and Aunty Kim?*
*Who's she or it or her or him?*
*I'm ninety-four, don't give a darn*
*I went to school inside a barn*
*From May to June to late November*

*Who you are I can't remember*
*PRONOUNS help me round the horn*
*Of table talk— You! Pass the corn!*


**PREPOSITION** (to be performed to/with a stuffed animal)

*My cat is on me, lucky me*
*Oh please get off me, off my knee!*
*Cat or self, the boundaries blur*
*You weigh so much, it's not just "fur"*
*You feed so much at dinner call*
*Your shape veers toward a basketball*
*And gassy is your air behind*
*So snuggling from afar is fine*
*But no— You're hurt, complain with meows*
*You won't accept more thens than nows*
*Cat on, cat off—these two conditions*
*Differ just by prepositions.*


**CONJUNCTION** (OMG—Valley Girl! could also be one of RuPaul's drag queens!)

*Oh my gawd, girl, have you heard?!?!*
*The latest dirt from period third?!?!?*
*So Pat and Kelly had a fight*
*That Brittany Olsen tried to right*
*But, bffs with Clare and Ann*
*And Beth and Lynn and Jane and Nan?*
*A catfight started in the yard!*
*And Brittany lost her Starbucks card!*
*The drama, in words I won't mince*

*Because, although, unless and since*
*Nouns connect with just conjunctions*
*And without her lattes, she can't function.*

**INTERJECTION** (rebel school boy: Max in *Where the Wild Things Are*)

*Yes! Great! Rad! Cool!*
*We're done with poems, assigned for school!*
*Ouch! Crikey! Fiddlesticks! Darn!*
*I yelled, "Huzzah!" and smacked my arm!*
*And spilled some root beer over this poem!*
*Now parts of speech are drowned in foam!*
*Interjections that rule the day*
*Are curse words that I dare not say*
*Although those words are dear to me*
*I turn those in? I get a D*
*My entire weekend, lost to grammar*
*So teacher! Please, ma'am? Rest your hammer.*

Grade? We are improving! B+! (Probably because the teacher sensed I wrote them, but we'll take it!) UC Merced wait list, here we come!

# "Summer"

## A "June" of One's Own

# Let's Commence

CHARLIE, THE GIRLS, and I are driving north up the coast, to Carmel Grove, for my nephew Sam's high school graduation.

We talk about how high school graduation will be different from any of the girls' previous ones, as in fact will their (fingers crossed) college graduations. Where there is a guest "commencement speaker."

"Like who?" Hannah asks.

"Like me!" I say. "I actually had to give a commencement speech once."

"No!" says Hannah.

Charlie says, "That's right, your mother did."

"It was at this little college in Orange County. From public radio, I was famous enough to be invited, but not famous enough that the graduates knew me."

"Henh?" Hannah asks.

"Let's put it this way. When you google 'Best Commencement Speeches,' which I did, all these web nerds will eagerly tell you that the best commencement speeches ever were made by Bono and Steve Jobs. Steve Jobs's speech described his fascination with Japanese calligraphy and how that led to Apple products' beautiful design. Bono's tasked an entire graduating class with making sure there's always clean drinking water in Africa. I think. I didn't finish it. I was too depressed."

"I don't get it," Hannah says.

"The point is, when you're a cultural rock star, you can say anything. Dare to dream! Dare to be different! Dare to dare! Sincerely, Oprah Winfrey. Regular people have to work harder. I literally tried googling 'How to Write a Commencement Speech for Regular People.'"

"My brother should google something like that," Charlie muses. "He's best man at a wedding next month. Those toasts can go wrong quickly. Suddenly the best man is drunkenly reminiscing about doing shots together in college and all the skanky girls the groom dated back in the day! Room goes dark—"

"'How to Write a Best Man Speech.'" Hannah has googled it on her phone. "Top search: 'How to Write a Best Man Speech When You Can't Stand the Bride.' Answer: 'Hire a comedian from our staff to ghostwrite it for you, it's that impossible.' So what do you write, mom?"

"Well, I said advice we give now will soon become obsolete, and then I kind of went the 'wear sunscreen' route. It was only eight minutes long. Essentially, I told the story of my own graduation in 1983. Our commencement speaker was novelist James Michener. The title of his speech was 'Your Revolution.'"

"What was your revolution?" Hannah asks.

"Something to do with space. Michener had just written a book about it. His hope was that our generation would pioneer manned space exploration to Mars and beyond."

"With the possible exception of Matthew McConaughey in *Interstellar*," Charlie says, "our generation has not done that."

"Right," I say. "I guess that makes us the Not So Great Generation. Fifty years since Neil Armstrong, we harness the computing power that once launched rockets in our cell phones. And use it to Yelp the nearest Cheesecake Factory."

Charlie: "And the guy pioneering space travel today is no astronaut or war hero or even a Nobel Prize winner, but Elon Musk—the guy who invented PayPal."

"Many of my Caltech physics classmates ended up doing statistical modeling for Wall Street or writing algorithms for beer gun pressure at Applebee's." I turn to Hannah. "That's why I have so little career advice for you."

Charlie agrees: "In *The Graduate*, remember? 'Plastics.'"

"Most trend lines suggest a boom in the field of gerontology. Look at caregiver Thomas. Your future college tuitions are pouring into your grandpa's GI tube."

"I remember my culmination!" Sally suddenly says.

"Into what?" Charlie asks.

"Sixth grade."

"Really?" Charlie rolls his eyes.

"I rolled my eyes, too," I say, "but actually it was cute. It was fun to see all these former kindergarteners now in their little ties and party dresses, semi-grown-up."

"We each gave a speech," Sally recalls.

"All seventy of them," I add. "It took two and a half hours."

"What do people even have to reminisce about when they're *ten*?" Charlie asks.

"Field trips—" Sally says wistfully.

"Right," I say. "Memorable ones obediently cited included the Griffith Observatory, Skirball, and something something 'adobe.' But the runaway favorite?"

"Second-grade whale watching!" Sally says.

"I also found you fifth graders very eager to thank the friends who pulled you through 'when times were tough.' Perhaps like when you realized your field trips peaked in second grade, with the whale watching, and from hence on, instead of the thrill of watching a classmate vomit over the side of the boat, you would only be visiting museums. Anyway. People would name their friends, from three to almost fifteen. I counted. The most thanked friend in your grade was someone named Yamillah."

Sally nods. "Yamillah was good people."

"And remember, Sally, you actually won that award!"

"What for?" asks Charlie.

Sally raises a "for Narnia" fist: "The Ellen Rubin Award for perfect attendance!"

"The PTA president posted a photo of Sally getting it on my Facebook page," I say. "It was like a shot of cocaine. Well-wishers flooded in for what one friend dubbed 'the Cal Ripkin of fifth grade.' Other families shared their own happy news. One friend reported that his own fifth grader had been voted 'most courteous.' Another couldn't resist adding that her own son—now nineteen—had once been voted 'most elegant' in kindergarten—here's the kicker—in France. Another shared the exciting news that her seven-month-old puppy had just learned to catch a ball. I was tempted to do a follow-up post—a photo of this most wonderful LAUSD award Sally also got—"

"What?" asks Charlie.

Sally can barely get it out: "Certificate of Achievement in the Area of Bus Riding for Improved Behavior on the Bus!"

We howl with laughter: "Literally true!"


"OH, NOW THE trees are starting . . ."

My daughters always find going to Carmel Grove a magical experience. It's another planet, compared to their hometown of Van Nuys.

Driving them home across Victory Boulevard, a tangle of telephone wires and exhaust, past the pupuserias, tire shops, and Yoshinoya beef bowls, I used to apologize for the fact that their parents were working artists, our neighborhood was butt ugly, an eyesore, and that we didn't have the money to raise them in a grassy enclave.

By contrast, Carmel Grove is one of those places—like Aspen, like Santa Barbara—that you get out of the plane or car and the blue sky hits you, slaps you in the face, like a young Michelle Pfeiffer in heels.

Not only that, Carmel Grove is an idyllic place of kindly protection. The wildlife is protected, the children are protected, even the elderly people are protected, striding healthfully through the grassy dunes in their Scandinavian sweaters.

In fact, it's so beautiful it scars you forever. It secretly makes you hate any place that isn't it—like your own home.

CG is on a hillock above the Pacific Ocean, which plunges away dramatically in a crash of emerald waves, puffy white clouds above, perfect today as it is every day.

Even the bakery we stop at is like an illuminated painting of pastries so aromatic they seem to exhale when we arrive, a silvery bell ringing behind.

Not to mention, at the local (nonchain) grocery store, there is an actual friendly local butcher. The meat is so pink and gleaming we can't help thinking that the animals were clearly happy, living in their own artistic commune, composing symphonies, before gently and humanely "transitioning" to continue to nurture us.

There is a church with a perfect steeple, a sloping hill in front so that you can almost see, with her elegant swan-like neck, Christina from the Wyeth painting *Christina's World*. We have to slow the car, for a moment, to let a trotting family of deer pass safely.

The late wife of my brother—Sam's father—picked out a beach house in the early 1990s for $300,000, which we thought was exorbitant. Suffice it to say, it's now worth much more than that. She was a teacher, he is an engineer—you can't even feel alienated by what has become a luxury piece of real estate. It's just Carmel Grove's gentle good luck.

SO HERE WE ARE at Sam's graduation. The sun is shining. Metal risers gleam.

There are festive balloons, leis, personalized graduation caps. The orchestra begins. "Pomp and Circumstance."

Here come a dozen girls in sundresses bearing flowers. Behind them march 150 beaming graduates.

The "Call to Colors" seems to confuse the two be-gowned boys bearing a flag and two white prop rifles. They stand for a moment, in a haze, as if confused. The action halts. The principal prompts them on mic. "Ahhh, Call to Colors. Stand tall for the flag. *Raise the flag.*"

I whisper to my crew, "That would never happen in Van Nuys. Our ROTC is really on top of it. You really need to be in L.A. for the good riflework."

Though if lacrosse sticks came to Van Nuys, people would be using them for spits to barbecue pork ribs of many nations.

I'm relieved our Sam doesn't look at all disemboweled by his college shutout. On the contrary, he's beaming and happy. "Who was on the Honor Roll—GPA 3.8 or above?" Apparently Sam was. He stands. "Who played varsity sports?" He stands. "Who played in the orchestra?" For two years, he played in the first violin section— toward the back, but still in first.

It is a lovely set of accomplishments. When had he had time to sleep halfway through the day like my girls?

Then come the speeches. Valedictorians and salutatorians. They fall into two categories.

First, valedictorian. Asian American, fearsome stats: 4.7 GPA, varsity fencing and swimming champion, Model Debate Squad, STEM honor something, 100,000 hours of community service. She's headed on scholarship to Stanford.

"Classmates!" Grace, the valedictorian, declares with an almost warlike intensity. She begins quoting from Robert Frost's "The Road Not Taken."

"Two roads diverged in a yellow wood . . . !" She goes on to say, I think, that the standard interpretation of the two roads suggests choosing safety(?), but a deeper interpretation invites one to get lost in the woods. Essentially, Grace is daring her classmates, in their Hawaiian leis and oversized yellow sunglasses, with plushy animals hanging over their graduation caps, to stop, to smell the flowers, to be themselves, to plunge into the unknown, to fail.

I can't help whispering to Charlie, "I feel it's ironic that Grace is challenging her classmates to fail because many of them have already. Next thing you know, Grace will be daring them to sleep in."

Because if there is anyone who had never failed, or slept in, it is Grace. It seems she hadn't had even a minute to fail, with her schedule and formidable train of extracurriculars.

By contrast I see Sam, next generation, looking up at her in total rapture. His face seems to say, "We're graduating!" I remember the boy who attacked with his king in chess, who loves riding bikes with his friends.

The salutatorian, a bean-pole boy with wiry hair, in a husky voice tinged with emotion, promises, "I will remember you, the faces at the lockers. We will never see each other again. This is a time that's now moving into the past."

The sun is setting. Golden hour. A palpable sigh comes over the crowd. There's the reading of the names.

"Ach!" I whisper to Charlie. "Why don't they *practice* the names first? Or say ahead of time, 'I may butcher your name, that's life,' but *then* don't do the hesitant questioning 'Patrizio . . . Oionoscola . . . Hahabjelay . . . ?' "

But everyone is thrilled, from the tubby short dude with Coke-bottle glasses, whose presence on stage draws a jubilant howl from forty teary people, to a tall thin girl with acne who draws less of a sound, the void into which the Loh family cheers, because we can't bear anyone not graduating to loud applause. It's our own version of "No Child Left Behind."

To say good-bye, among a mind-boggling fluorescence of pool toys, leis, and sunglasses, the graduates throw off their caps into the twilight.

And just for one moment, one safe space, one wormhole in time, the families drift off glazed-eyed, sated with joy.

"I can't wait to graduate from high school," Hannah murmurs in awe, as if it's a magical possibility she has just thought of for the very first time.

"I'm scared to graduate," says Sally. "I'm going to miss every-one. My friends, my teachers, my locker . . . I still miss Yamillah!" she half-wails.

"From fifth grade?" I ask.

"Yes," Sally says, "she was good people." But even as she says this, behind her glasses, her eyes gleam as they follow the balloons lifting, lifting in the sky.

And I glimpse a worldview of both commencements and endings, where both sadness and joy exist at once. And for a moment, we dwell not amid the chronological march of history—the decades, the movements, the milestones—but in the humble craft of the family, small, not legendary, taking a thing in, in a breath.

# Can't Think of Anything Clever to Say about "July"

# 101 (If You Count Each Piece of "Extra" Checked Baggage) Arguments Against "Summer Fun"

## (A Wee Rant/Digression)

I ALWAYS THINK I want to travel and to do "fun things" in summer, but there are really so many reasons not to—at least in America. (I should really be wine tasting in Provence, but that would be in an alternate universe.) Let me count the ways.

**1. Kids in pools—a violation.**

I was at a hotel last summer, reading a book, squeak of the gate, and like a too-gaudy Olympic opening ceremony from some desperate Third World country, a surreal parade of gigantic inflatable pool toys marches in. There's a green T-Rex, a purple unicorn with fluttering eyelashes, a tropical yellow palm tree, and an eight-foot-long hot dog.

*What's next?* you think. *A giant gall bladder topped by a maraschino cherry?*

All these dirigibles were there for one reason: extremely loud and frantic water racing. "One, two, three, go!" the children screamed. Piercing shrieks as four tidal waves hit. An hour later, exhausted from their time trials, the shriekers floated to the pool's shallow end, spent. They flung their deflating toys over the side onto the lawn. A

shaky silence falls over their pool toy graveyard. And then: "Marco."
"Polo." "MARCO!" "POLO!"

## 2. "Amusement" parks of any form—the humiliation.

One time, Charlie took me and the girls to this amusement park
called "The Fun Spot." It was a terrifying Erector Set of roller coast-
ers, elevator drops, screaming. Because I hate thrill rides, Charlie
suggests we start with a very small Ferris wheel. It is so dinky, in the
gondola ahead of us are two elderly Muslim ladies in headscarves and
glasses. They grip the rail, looking anxious. Poor things. It's probably
their first time in an amusement park. But no, as soon as the gondola
lifts, while I have a panic attack, the elderly Muslim ladies raise their
hands above their heads and cackle! One takes a selfie! I renamed it
"The Vomit Spot."

But now I see it—a small, fenced-in enclosure with "kiddie
rides." Instead of the ominously named "Riddler's Revenge," here
are G-rated rides like "The Happy Swing!" Two feet off the ground
and moving at five miles an hour, these rides are perfect for me.
Except that their cartoon elephant-shaped seats are way too small for
a middle-aged person's butt. But wait—it turns out some come with a
special "fat seat." Determined to have some "fun," I strap myself into
a vertical bouncer called "The Frog Hopper." I'm fine until it raises us
eight feet into the air. I grip the rails and scream, triggering laughter
from four-year-olds. Next comes a tiny roller coaster literally in the
shape of a snail. My biggest fear is that the metal safety bar is going
to bruise my shins as we careen slowly in circles.

## 3. Calculating "air miles"—how to provoke a brain aneurysm.

A couple of months ago, I'm trying to book a trip with United Air
miles. But they're the wrong kind of miles. But then I see an ad for
Spirit Air! Amazing price—but you can't take a carry-on bag. For a

full week, my daughters and I, all three of us, will each need a carry-on bag— But wait! This thought actually crosses my mind. What if we FedEx boxes of our clothes ahead? Sure, our Cleveland family friends might not appreciate receiving FedEx boxes of our clothes. But geez, Spirit is charging—what?—$50 a bag? Three people on two flights—that's $300 more— Unless we just fly our clothes one way, wear them, then toss them into Lake Erie— But wait, for just $59 per year, you can join the Spirit Air $9 bag club—!

Like a whipped dog, I return to my captor, United. And suddenly, I discover that I can reserve three tickets at 30 percent off under a program called Basic Economy. You might ask: "Why so cheap?"

The next day, United sends me a "morning after" e-mail that asks—and this is a direct quote: "Do you realize what you've done?" In Basic Economy, not only do you not get a carry-on bag, families are not seated together. Doesn't need a change of clothes, flying alone— Who's the target customer here? A time-traveling eighteenth-century serial killer? And how does breaking up families save United money? It's as if they're saying, sure, 30 percent off, but:

We can't guarantee you'll land in Cleveland.
We can't guarantee you a seat that hasn't been peed on.
We can't guarantee you won't be handed a crying baby.

4. **"Bargain" car rental agencies from which one might catch an infection.**
"Kayak"-ing the white water rapids of cheap car rentals, on that same trip, I'd found a company called ACE, offering a tiny car that looked like a Yugo. Upon arrival, I find out why. Our instructions? Walk past the Ground Transportation counter, get into "lane four," then turn left and walk half a mile, past all the Avis, Budget, and Enterprise signs and wait, literally, and I quote, "under the sign that is blank."

"I know that we're not Platinum members of anything," I grouse to my daughters, "but standing under a blank sign? Can ACE at least not tape their logo up there? It's so humiliating!"

"Maybe they didn't have enough money to commission a logo," says Hannah.

### 5. "Breakfast" does not count as a "life hack."
Two years ago, Charlie and I stayed at a Residence Inn. Meaning it's both a residence *and* an inn. Plus, a Marriott. It is, in short, a kind of "Staybridge." I literally have no idea what I just said.

But no. Stepping into the RI at the M is like entering a futuristic, Euro-styled planet. Here are white modular fireplaces blazing in midsummer. Art Deco lamps that have BELIEVE printed on them in twelve languages. Pulsing in the background is a catchy music video: *Take Residence at Residence Inn*, set to Zeroleen's rappy "All Good" as hip, racially diverse Silicon Valley twentysomethings gambol through the facilities. They arise, don Untuckit shirts, breakfast on granola and kiwi, Skype on their MACs, clink imported beers, shoot hoops— Yes, there's basketball on site.

But the lie is revealed the next morning at breakfast. There are no hipsters there. Just Middle American vacationers who don't understand breakfast. Instead of little boxes of Special K, there are clear plexiglass towers of cereal. It's not immediately obvious how to get the cereal out. Using our knowledge of pet feeders, we eventually intuit that you place your bowl underneath, open a drawer, and cereal rushes out. There are copious cereal piles where other guests have discovered that the hard way.

We now venture near the glowing red bagel-toasting machine. A frantic hand-lettered sign responds to what was clearly a previous traumatic incident: PLEASE DO NOT PUT YOUR HAND INSIDE THE TOASTER. VERY HOT! On to the waffle-making station. It seems to require pouring batter into a tiny cup, emptying the cup onto a hot waffle iron, and flipping it in thirty seconds—? Sure! Batter is dripping everywhere—we and other bumbling guests do our best to sop it up with napkins—the station now resembles a waffle slaughterhouse. It's clear: none of us is going to be giving a TED Talk any time soon. To my right, a teen girl unapologetically stirs honey into hot chocolate. Her T-shirt says RUNNING ON DR PEPPER AND DRY SHAMPOO. Her dad, in sun visor, sports a T-shirt that reads THIS IS HOW IT'S DONE.

**6. A "Carnival Cruise" is neither "carnival" nor "cruise."**
But here is the nadir of everything Charlie and I have ever done. One time, maddened by the searing heat of summer, Charlie and I lost our minds via some sort of strange Groupon deal and decided to go on a Carnival Cruise. It was so cheap, it was almost cheaper than staying at home. But the emotional cost! Talk about Third World.

To get to the ship, you enter a large astrodome thing in Long Beach. It is fluorescent-lit, a vast interplanetary Greyhound Bus Station. Once in line, it's like a "DMV on the Sea." There are men in cargo shorts, flip-flops, baseball hats, sunglasses rotated around to the back of the head. There are kids standing in floaties on dry land. In these families, literally three out of five people have tattoos. There are big Asian men with tattoos across the backs of their meaty calves. Skinny white girls whose fresh tattoos suppurate across their backs and shoulders.

Upon entering the bowels of the ship, now comes a light latrine smell. More horrible is, you seem to be in the bowels of a windowless casino several neon floors high. The décor is garish in a way Las Vegas doesn't even seem to be any more. Even Las Vegas is seeing natural fibers and a new fusion cuisine by Wolfgang Puck. This was hot pink and turquoise and a color I might like to call "insane magenta."

There were these fake metallic kind of Roman godheads everywhere and fake gold Egyptian sphinxes.

Swallowing revulsion, we are directed to our stateroom on God knows what level (Lido level, Promenade level, Disney Prince in Rocky Horror fishnet stockings level), which is like four faux-gold-crusted miles away down a windowless mole tunnel. Our smallish "stateroom" has a smeary metal porthole and undecorated gray walls. Upon entry I feel claustrophobic. I'm not going to make it. I'm literally going to have to sleep up on deck somewhere. I am fighting panic and rising nausea.

We go to the "Lido Café" for "lunch." As we walk in—neon disco lights flashing above us—we understand what was meant by Charlie's mom Tweedie, a veteran of many cruises (think Holland and Norwegian lines), when she exclaimed, "You're going on a *Carnival* Cruise? You'll never cruise again!"

Charlie had laughed at that, and packed several "jackets" for "dinner." Now he's eerily quiet.

There are heat lamps over tureens of gluey brownish slop, optimistically known as "chicken piccata." The bright spot is we can take our plates outside. True, there are nets over the side of the ship to literally keep us from being attacked by seagulls, but we do have the place to ourselves. Almost all of the large tattooed people prefer to eat inside, perhaps working on their "fry tans."

I had pictured sinking into a warm pool overlooking the Pacific and being handed a blended drink. After "lunch," we ascend to the supposedly sunbathing-friendly "Promenade" deck. There are more heat-lamp stations of greasy food, deafening music—you know that calypso tune that goes "Hot, hot, hot"?—and, just beyond a sea of deck chairs, a small pool bisected into even smaller pools, almost kiddie pools. It is—get this—completely drained, covered by a net, and posted with signs that say POOL CLOSED.

Gum-chewing cruise personnel direct us instead to the Serenity deck, an adults-only corner at the back of the boat with two medical-sized Jacuzzis. The Jacuzzis are filled with beer-swilling seventeen-year-olds and their patriarch, pro-NRA Dad. Pro-NRA Dad soliloquies loudly about his guns and hunting and how Candy, his wife, cried when she put the deer down "with all the blood." Everyone clinks beers in hysterics, including, apparently, Candy. It is a warm family story.

On the next level is a boutique selling hellacious trinkets and duty-free CÎROC orange vodka. There's a hellacious "art auction" with some truly terrifying paintings—you know, sharks in pink lipstick playing poker.

In case you were wondering, yes, the biggest discussion Charlie and I had before boarding the ship was about alcohol consumption. Carnival was touting the forty-five-dollars-a-day "Cheers!" beverage plan, where your drinks were free, up to fifteen cocktails a day.

Cawed a young woman in heart-shaped Barbie sunglasses next to me, the second day at 1 p.m., "Oh my God! The drink limit is fifteen and he said I have just four to go!" Plastic cups clicked in celebration.

I will not end up going into a pool once in four days. Even when they put water back into the pools, there's no room. The twin Jacuzzis around the tiny bisected pool are in constant churn. The signs say MAX OCCUPANCY 13, even though each can barely seat eight. That said, at several points, in amazement, I count eighteen humans per spa.

Granted, several are children on laps, whose heads will disappear underwater for minutes at a time. Like whack-a-moles. Life is cheap!

Because there is no lifeguard on duty. The pool sign says DEPTH 4 FEET: ABSOLUTELY NO DIVING. And yet, there is *so* much diving. Particularly by the fortysomething dads, man-breasts jiggling. Later there will be a "hairy chest contest," with men running about in drag and doing suggestive booby dances for lady volunteers.

So of course the only way to get through these four days is TO DRINK HEAVILY. Our third day begins with a Bloody Mary, for breakfast, at nine, lunch, white wine, a martini to unwind after, drop an edible around two . . . and that's when I finally lose it. I feel reality swimming before me, like I am in an IMAX movie theater, seated in the dark, and the 3-D "reality" of Carnival Cruise is floating before me.

That night, we will end up singing karaoke. We will join the waitstaff in celebrating a birthday by singing and dancing, "Ce-le-bration time, come ON!"

Though weirdly, as Charlie pointed out later, "We did not fight."

# July 4th-ish

B UT CAN SUMMER get worse? It can.
Time has passed. The wounds have healed. I can finally talk
about my fourth of July.

On the one hand, as a divorced mother? I'm frankly delighted
not to have to spend the fourth of July with my family, your family,
or anyone's family.

This is the time of year my ex-husband Ben takes the girls to Minnesota for lake fishing at his family's cabin. I celebrate them all: Ben's
perfectly nice family, all the friendly Midwestern fisher folk raising
icy Pabst Blue Ribbons, and the plentiful and delicious walleye. That
said, I'm just as happy to make space for others to share the sandy
bunks, the swarmy bugs, and the ankle bites—so-o-o many bites.

That said, the divorced mother's question remains: On the fourth
of July, what the hell should I do?

I'm discussing this with my friend Trayce, another divorced mom.

"This is the time of year when, oh, the ranks close," she agrees.
"Our married parent friends all disappear into their families, driving
to see the grandparents in San Diego, or similar."

"Our childless gay male friends should be a help, but they also go silent to our frantic texts as they disappear into fabulous parties in the hills, having been at this family-free fourth thing longer than we have."

"Exactly. They're keeping us divorced moms—the weeds—out of their carefully husbanded ecosystems."

Not to face the lone hibachi with a single skinless chicken breast and a tumbleweed, we made a pact that if either of us get wind of any barbecue—good, bad, or ugly—we will invite the other person.

Last week of June goes by. Nothing.

July 1st, July 2nd . . .

On July 3rd, at 8 p.m., glass of wine in hand, I type an e-mail:

*Dear Very Close Small Circle of Friends\* to Whom We Are Not Ashamed to Admit We Have Absolutely No 4th of July Plans,*

*If you either can't decide amongst your BULGING COR-NUCOPIA of 4th invites or if you too came up bupkis, join us at 5 for cocktails. And eventually some BBQ. If you have any other 4th of July orphans they are welcome; if you are horrified that we have extended such a last-minute invite, please delete this e-mail and forget you ever saw it.*

\*A lie. I have opened the e-mail circle wide to guess at ANY SIN-GLETONS WHO MIGHT BE ALONE on the fourth of July. It is a Rogues' Gallery of C and D guests.

WITHIN A MINUTE OF hitting "send," I get an e-mail back from my friend Paula. I'm thrilled! Paula is a wonderful person I haven't seen in ages because she has been single-mothering her daughter—who is now eighteen and off to college! Reunion time!

But no.

"Oh my gosh," she writes back. "I was just about to invite you to a last-minute thing I've suddenly decided to host, a picnic and wine and hike to see the fireworks over Santa Monica!"

"Dang!" I write back. "That sounds much more fun than what we're doing—huddling in a landlocked backyard full of dead leaves and tumbleweeds. But you didn't invite me on time, did you?"

"I didn't have your old Compuserve e-mail. Who's still on Compuserve? Trouble is, I don't have quite enough people. I have a painfully shy JPL engineer with a nerdy math teacher from my daughter's old school plus my cousin Barbara who literally IS a nun plus this droopy guy I met on match dot com—no sparks but I always feel sorry for him over the holidays. I'm going to hide in the kitchen and drink myself into a Bolivian." She literally types "a Bolivian."

"Sounds better than my guest list," I write. "It looks like my married couple friends Will and Annalise just now RSVP'ed with their angry twenty-year-old son, who still lives at home. Oh, and look at this—my perennially depressed fifty-two-year-old bachelor friend Frank is coming. He is absolutely euphoric to be invited and is bringing FIGS, FIGS, FIGS—all in CAPS! This is going to be the barbecue from hell!"

JULY 4TH 8 A.M.

Charlie has cut short his usual morning forty-five-minute-minimum reading session of the *New York Times*. This literally never happens. But momentous events are in play today. Charlie is launching a gigantic BBQ project.

It's Cochinita Pibil, cooked in actual banana leaves. The complicated *New York Times* recipe he has printed out appears to be five single-spaced pages long, with multiple breakout sections. It looks as complex as a Bach oratorio. It's supposed to take four hours, but last time he tried, it took eight, so he's trying to aim for nine.

Trayce arrives at three to help set up. She's looking festive in a yellow sundress and strappy red sandals. She puts bags down on the kitchen counters.

"Where's Charlie?"

I point out the kitchen window. We see the bottom half of a pale humanoid—pink Bermuda shorts and lime tennis shoes—struggling under a cloud of white smoke.

"We won't see him for a while," I say. "He's having a little trouble with the coals."

"Low-carb mojitos." Trayce licks lime off her finger, hands me a glass. We clink, sip. They're fabulous!

Our moods immediately go to festive.

"Until my divorce," Trayce says, "I never realized how much I've always absolutely hated the fourth of July. The awful family 'event' of it!"

" 'Independence' Day?" I agree. "It's actually the exact opposite!"

"Exactly!" she says. "Fourth of July is huge crowds, parking miles away from a crowded beach, a poop accident, an ice cream scoop tumbling to the ground, wet children in shivering wet swimsuits that you'll end up carrying, one-by-one, like potato sacks across searing asphalt (flip-flops left on the wrong side of the parking lot or washed away in a rising tide), the shrieking and tears when the fireworks are, like gunshots, *too loud*."

"Oh oh oh," I say. "The other day, I was in Target and it struck me how many summer toddler items—swimsuits, sandals, water wings—are *incredibly brightly colored*. Like poisonous frogs in nature. Bright colors hypnotize sleep-deprived mothers into thinking that summers with children are actually fun."

"It's so the opposite!" Trayce exclaims. "It's packing them into the car with all of their endless beach shit—the bathing suits, towels, sunglasses, sunscreen, juice boxes, and . . . ominous drum roll . . . *swim diapers*."

"Oh my God. The swim diapers!"

"If you can't control your bowels?" Trayce waves her mojito. "Guess what? Forget the freedom of 'Independence' Day. You don't *get* to swim."

"What's next? A little American flag on a . . . baby snorkel catheter?"

But then again, the way the evening unfolded, it almost made us nostalgic for the horrors of actual children, as opposed to adult-shaped children.

Which is to say, at promptly 5:45, the Island of Misfit Toys starts arriving.

The Gentlemen Callers trickle in. Jerry pairs a red kilt with a Bob Marley T-shirt. Tex brings a mysterious Serbian girlfriend named Svetlana, all in black. Bradford is in a white eye patch. Never explained.

Carol, a poetess and physical therapist, has brought her small Pekingese in a plaid carrying case. There is much disturbing licking of each other's faces. Carol has been dating, and things are not going well.

"I was messaging with this guy on Match.com," she says, "but he was always suggesting a quick coffee near his home at odd times of the day, never evenings. It eventually comes out that he still lives with his ex because he can't afford to move. He said it's called a 'stayparation.' A stayparation—is that a thing?"

Charlie seems to have calmed his coals but still looks worried. Julia and Andie arrive.

Frank arrives, his dress shirt soaked in sweat, with FIGS, FIGS, FIGS! Assessing the food, I see that someone should have hostessed this party.

The potluck items include meat, meat, meat, chips, a lopsided strawberry pie, a very sweaty salad with way too many ingredients, and FIGS, FIGS, FIGS!

"When will dinner be ready?" Carol asks worriedly. "Mr. Pimpernel"—her dog, apparently—"is hungry."

"Charlie?" I yell out, toward the backyard, engulfed in white swirling smoke (does that mean the cardinals have picked a pope?). "What time do you think the food will be ready?"

"Hard to say," he replies. "I'm still having some . . . trouble with my coals!"

Because it's so hot, people are drinking without hydrating. . . . They're getting increasingly agitated. The sky darkens to a murky brown dusk.

And now here it comes. Ranting, both energetic and futile, about politics. The place where all party conversations go to die.

"Have you heard?" Carol says, feeding little Mr. Pimpernel meat off the table. She nods sagely. "He's building ovens."

"What?"

"Do you read J. C. Yewell—you know, the writer?" None of us do. "It's what he said in this amazing op-ed here on Facebook." Carol proffers her phone. "There's a list, for the ovens, and the Jews are going first."

"I think if I were Muslim I would be more scared," counters Andie. "Or Mexican, for that matter."

"Maybe we should just get off Facebook for five minutes and stop hyperventilating," Trayce says.

To which Carol ominously murmurs: "That's what they said in Germany."

"What did they say?" Julia asks.

"'Blah, blah, blah. Take a rest! Get off Facebook! Stop hyperventilating!'"

"Carol, I'm concerned as you," Trayce says, "but I'm pretty sure they didn't have Facebook. So that can't be exactly what they said in Germany."

Carol shakes her head. "That's what they said."

" 'That's what they said in Germany' is what they said in Germany? It's not even in German."

"What about the Russians!" Jerry shouts, from the grill area.

"Oh God," I wail. "Can we have one party not ruined by political talk? It's fucking July!"

Tex's date Svetlana, in her dark turtleneck, drinking a mystery drink that Tex keeps refilling, rises on our porch like a daimoness. Thick Russian accent.

"Let me tell you Serbian joke. So, Satan is sitting around hell being bored—"

Tex: "Satan jokes are great, aren't they? Quick Satan joke from the *New Yorker*. Satan is giving a tour of hell. He says, 'The good news is there are four meals a day. The bad news is that they're all continental breakfast.' "

"Hm," says Svetlana. "So, Satan is sitting around hell being bored. Around him are former dictators Nicolai Ceauşescu, Saddam Hussein, and Slobodan Milošević. They want to phone their former countries, to check in, see how their people are doing. The devil charges them accordingly: One million for two minutes to Romania, two million for two minutes to Iraq.

"When it comes to Milošević's two minutes to Serbia, however, the cost is surprisingly nothing. Why?

" 'This is local call,' Satan says. 'Hell to hell.' " A beat.

Tex: "As opposed to Americans, for whom hell is continental breakfast!"

Svetlana inhales her cigarette, crushes it out.

"Horrible leaders get elected around the world every day. Now for the first time, you know how other countries feel. Get over yourselves."

Andie is cutting and sorting figs like a madwoman. "The midterm elections. It's all about—"

Svetlana: "You're spoiled in California! If you open your fridge and food is there, revolution is not going to happen."

Carol suddenly bursts into tears. Her dog starts yapping. I am looking for a Bolivian to drink myself into.

Shouts erupt.

Charlie and Jerry are arguing, heatedly, about grilling.

Jerry: "Michael Pollan says that's exactly where you shouldn't place the coals—"

Charlie yells back: "Michael Pollan? Are you kidding? That's some kind of fucked-up Williamsburg shit!"

"What's that smell?" Julia asks suddenly.

"What smell?" I ask.

Andie looks at Julia intently. "It's like . . . smoky."

"Burning? Is something burning?" Julia asks.

"Oh my God!" Carol screams suddenly, in a high-pitched voice. "Fire!" Immediately, Mr. Pimpernel's yapping turns into shrieking, as though he himself is being spitted on a hot skewer.

And indeed, there is crackling, smoldering, small orange flames flicker from the carpet of dead leaves in our yard—the perfect summer kindling.

Everyone now is screaming and tumbling toward the BBQ area—except for Carol, who is trying to rush inside the house with her dog. . . . But she has so many complicated bags and satchels, now a water bottle is rolling, a vial of pills has splattered open. . . . "Call 911!" she screams. "Call 911!"

My phone is God knows where, so I step into the kitchen to try the landline. Because we get so many robocalls, it's disconnected. "Where's the power cord?" I yell. "Charlie? Where's the cord?"

Bradford is—what? He is spraying his beer all over a bouquet of flames, hopping back and forth on his feet as though it were a tribal dance.

"Dude! Don't do that. That only makes it worse!" Jerry yells at him.

"A blanket! What about a blanket?" Tex exclaims, rushing toward the flames with—

"No!" I scream. "Not that blanket! That's my grandmother's!"

Svetlana has her head thrown back and is cackling like a witch: "HAHAHAHAHA! The American apocalypse! Bombs burst in mid-air!" She lifts her iPhone and begins to take selfies of herself, fire in the back.

The howl of fire trucks begins— Neighbors gather and look over our fence— If only swim diapers would have cut it! Worst BBQ ever!

# A Very Hindu Audit

IN THE MAILBOX. A thick 8½" × 11"-sized letter from the IRS.

Tearing it open, I see it's an Official Summons. There's a swirl of letters and numbers and line items. I feel seasick. The IRS claims some entity named "Sandra Loh" owes $5,000 in back taxes from 2015. The IRS is going to disallow an extra $25,000 in business expenses—$25,000, is that what I claimed? They're adding a hefty penalty, multiplied by 597 days or weeks—

Bottom line: The IRS wants $34,000.

I have ten days to respond.

The knees buckle. I grasp the counter. Feel for my phone. Dial my Bears. Three rings, then there are the telltale tritones: one-two-three! "This number has been disconnected."

No. I type an emergency e-mail. A second. A third. PLEASE RESPOND IMMEDIATELY!!! Nothing.

In disbelief, I drive to my tax accountants' Glendale Spanish palace. Something's amiss. There's the flutter of plastic tarping. Distant whine of a sander. The windows are open. Workmen are hammering.

I peer in. Through the front window, where Jacques's desk used to be, there is only dusty flooring, walls, and not a ceiling lamp but a light socket with a wire twisting out of it like on *CSI*.

I HAVE TO CALL Charlie's accountant, the former child actor. "Hamm, Carruthers and Associates."

Wow—they pick up before the second ring!

I've been prisoner in a CPA gulag for so many years, I'm startled to get an actual person on the phone, first try. My spirits lift a little.

Harold Hamm gets on the phone. He has a hearty, booming voice—think Ted Baxter in *The Mary Tyler Moore Show*.

I explain my frightening situation and he exclaims, "No problem! It's likely just a formality. Routine. You come in and I'll walk you through it."

"SEE?" CHARLIE SAYS. "You're going to be fine. Harold is great. Can I get you something while I'm up?"

Charlie is being extra nice to me, because I had forgotten that I had promised him that around this time, we would house five Hindu monks for five days.

Let's back up.

Once a year, Charlie's Hindu Indian mother "Amma," whose photograph he chants to, makes a trip to Los Angeles to see her L.A. devotees. She travels with a road crew: they do all the physical labor of setting up tents, prepping ritual objects (flowers, fruit, ghee), and running a traveling bookstore.

Charlie has gradually moved from straight devotee into volunteer producer for the organization. Because typically the crew has to stay at hotels in neighboring cities, whereas our house is just five minutes away from the venue, our hosting them would be a huge spiritual boon.

"They'll sleep in the attic," Charlie says, "and you know the schedule they keep. They work fourteen hours a day. They'll never be in. They eat nothing but chia seeds. Talk about low maintenance."

It's true: it would be hard to imagine more serene and lovely men. Picture sensitive-eyed, quiet-voiced Caucasian gentlemen ranging from thirty-two to seventy-two in gauzy white pajamas. Beards are long, hair is buzzed, wildly frizzy, or wound up in lyrical man buns/topknots. They're the opposite of "bros."

"Besides," Charlie assures me, "they'll bring good tax karma."


HAROLD HAMM IS A large, rangy man in his seventies with a bald dome and massive cheekbones. By looks, he could have played a TV cowboy.

By some miracle, my 2015 tax return was still in the bank box under the stairwell where I left it. I slide it over to him. I fear he will open it and burst into laughter.

He glances over it, nods, and declares, "Everything looks good."

"Really?" I cry out in—frankly—disbelief.

"Listen," he says, "I could go with you to the audit, but in my experience we'll be better off if you go in alone."

"Oh, really?" I'm disappointed.

"Oh no, honey, if I go in," he gestures to himself, eyebrows up, "it'll be a pissing match with the IRS agent. Dog-eat-dog. But you, missy, with all your theater experience?" His voice drops to a silken purr. "You're our secret weapon."

I feel the same twinge I felt when being designated a gifted child, in first grade. He gets up from his desk and paces, thoughtful.

"An audit is a performance. If the IRS senses fear, they play on it. So when the agent talks to you, listen. Nod. Breathe. Don't react. Don't blink too much. Don't rush in with extra information. You take your receipts and page through them de-li-be-ra-tely. Like so."

Harold is clearly savoring his role as Method Acting tax audit auteur.

"Imagine you're coming in with your props, and your motions with these props are your 'business.'"

He starts making notes on yellow Post-its and sticking them all over my return. "So. Create different envelopes, for each different category, that you then label. Very simple. Meals, Travel, Gas. . . ."

"Meals, Travel, Gas," I repeat, like a mantra.

"You're getting it. You've got it!"

His voice is calming. Like some new Scientology trainee, I am feeling hypnotized into wild accounting optimism. This on-the-spectrum work is my métier; I'm going to win this; I'm going to kill this; I will get a 100 percent/A+ in tax auditry.

"To this you add any bills you have, receipts, records, a date book—"

"I'm so grateful you agreed to see me!" I burst out. "Because as I said—"

He waggles his finger: "In L.A., it's very common for CPAs to flee without a trace. They just don't want to do it anymore. They want to go to a beach somewhere."


CHARLIE CASUALLY TELLS ME that Amma's organization has sent some guidelines on how to properly house a Hindu crew, what Vedic practices, and Vastu, should be followed.

"Say what?"

"It's totally simple," he assures me. Men and women are supposed to sleep on separate floors and have separate bathrooms. Easy. The monks will be up in the attic on air mattresses. As my girls are spending the week with their dad, the second floor hall bathroom will be female-free. Phew.

Although we'll rarely see them, it's noted that the monks all follow a strict Ayurvedic diet.

"I can make curries!" Charlie exclaims, thrilled at the idea of a complicated new food project. "Slow-cooker curries!"

"But look here," I tap the list, "aside from no meat, 'meditation food' also means no dairy, onions, mushrooms, garlic—"

"No garlic?" He frowns. He can barely make cinnamon toast without garlic.

"Anything that grows in the ground is supposed to be unclean. Instead of butter, you must use ghee—"

"I would use it anyway—"

"Even tofu can be 'estrogenic.' Oh! You know what food is perfect?"

"What?"

"The—what is it?—Asian mung bean."

I find myself becoming oddly charmed by this project—intrigued by the challenge. Though they haven't asked, just in case they need a bite in the morning, I create a breakfast attic "prep" station. So the boys can be blissfully separate from unclean female me and my coffee. It's a white IKEA shelf of Whole Foods ancient grains, flaxseeds, trail mix, fruit. In the mini-fridge is rice milk, almond milk, and coconut milk. On impulse I've bought mini packets of raisins because it seemed they had some kind of Vedic symbol on them, as opposed to being stamped with the lowly Sun-Maid Raisins girl.

All is set.

What could go wrong?

. . .

"NAMASTE! NAMASTE!" Julien, Peter, Scott, and Shakti put their hands together and bow. They carry in their duffle bags from three large white cargo vans temporarily parked in our driveway. They are all here except Tavasha, the head monk, an intense thirtysomething man with waist-length hair. He is traveling tonight to Ojai with Amma for a special moon celebration, though his bag is being brought in.

Charlie shyly offers them some Ayurvedic Asian mung bean curry, which he went to fair lengths to make. However, as predicted, no one can stay to eat, as they need to prep a meditation site for the early-morning (6 a.m.?) session.

And off they go.

"Well, that was easy," I say.

Charlie looks a little disappointed, but we eat some of the Asian mung bean curry. It tastes slightly like mucus, although not in a bad way. We're in bed by ten.

Mid-dream, I hear a burst of what sounds like a sea of monks chanting—"manga, manga, manga"—over a very lo-fi radio.

I look at the clock. It's 3:00 a.m.

"Charlie," I whisper.

"What?" he rolls over.

"Manga, manga, manga—" Twenty seconds later, it stops.

"What was that?" I whisper.

"I don't know."

Silence again. I drift off.

And then it starts again—"manga, manga, manga" . . . I roll over to look at the clock. 3:15.

Then again, it stops.

"I think it's some kind of cell phone alarm," Charlie says, in wonder.

In Tavasha's bag, we realize. Tavasha, who is in Ojai. He notoriously never picks up his phone. Now we know why—it's not always on his corporeal self.

"It's probably for 3 a.m. meditation," Charlie says. "Amma says that's the perfect time."

"3 a.m.? When do they sleep?"

"Who needs sleep? I find it relaxing, don't you?" Charlie says, hugging me, although he may in fact be gently squeezing me into submission, like a boa constrictor.

So this continues. Lulled by the Ayurvedic Asian mung bean stew, I eventually drop off into my own meditation. In my case, it's a dream where I'm pulling some kind of rickshaw through India, with Judi Dench on my back in full beekeeper regalia eating Sun-Maid Raisins.

In the morning, as my daughters' bathroom shower vigorously thrums (monks shower for a long time—perhaps it's their only allowed physical pleasure in the day?), I pad downstairs to get coffee.

In the middle of the living room, I'm startled to see Julien, standing on his head, doing his morning yoga.

In the kitchen, Scott is tending to some smelly tea he's brewing. Peter is preparing a small flotilla of avocado toasts. The avocados are his, but the toast is our regular Oroweat bread from the basket. Hm.

Apparently Shakti consumes nothing. "As a breatharian, I live on air. I don't need food," he is saying, his calm smile framed by gray Jesus hair. A native of Portland, Shakti could be 65 or 35—if the 35-year-old had not slept for decades and long had his face encased in hot wax. "I get my energy from sunlight, man. It's Prana."

Charlie sees me and spins around.

"Good morning! Here's your coffee!" he sings out, like a cat caught with a bird. Or in this case, a cat caught in his own new personal set of white floaty man pajamas.

Scott turns to me and bows, offering me a pear.

"It is prasad, blessed by Amma, for your generosity. Namaste."

"Oh," I say, flattered.

And within the hour, thankfully, crunch of gravel, the three vans roll out.

With a sigh, I sit at the dining room table. I spread out my notes from my can-do meeting with Harold Hamm.

I look at my notes, and the return, and the Post-its, and realize . . . something is not clicking.

Without my inspiring mentor, my guru, my very own Tony Robbins of accounting, I don't actually truly understand the envelope system. The problem is, there isn't just one set of categories. There are two and three sets, from various sections of the return. If you mapped them out they would make intersecting Venn diagrams. So one receipt might actually want to live in three, or three and a half, different envelopes, possibly of different sizes. And geometries. Am I making sense to you?

I get up to fetch my records. I discover, due to the "Luz-cleaning-out-the-hallway-shelves" project, that the shelves where I've kept my personal records are . . . empty.

I start to hyperventilate.

"Calm down," I tell myself, as though I were that lady in *Gaslight*. "You can print out your United VISA miles statement for the whole year. In categories!"

After frantically typing in three sets of passwords I cannot remember (high school mascot: "Victor Viking"?), I am in! 2015! There it is! Bam! The printer starts printing. It stops. Why? The tiny Wi-Fi icon appears to be straining.

In slow motion, I scan the room and notice many open lap-

tops around me, next to small piles of trail mix and nuts and other
squirrel-type items.

The monks.

I make a muffled screaming sound.

Mr. White Floaty Pajamas—Professor Moonbeam—floats by,
conspicuously sipping some smelly tea.

"Can I *help* you?" Charlie asks.

"Yes!" I exclaim. "Please!"

"What can I do?"

I throw my hands up.

"If I could *describe* what to do, I would. That is the problem.
I can't even get my mind around this thing's gestalt." My voice is
skreeking. "It's like this, this thing! With envelopes! And Post-its!!"

"Relax," Charlie intones, illumined from within by pure sunlit
Prana. "It's an audit. No big deal."

"A $34,000 tax bill is no big deal?"

"They're just trying to scare you," he says, waving his white-
sleeved arm like a butterfly. "These IRS guys are losers. They've got
nothing better to do."

"How are they 'losers'?" I wonder. "They actually work for a
living." *Unlike many men currently sleeping in this building*, I think,
but do not say.

"They'll be amazed if you even show up," Charlie scoffs. "That's
what Bradford says. You shove a box of receipts at them and say, 'It's
your problem!' "

Oh my God.

Here are the various stages of Help I Would Appreciate from My
Partner:

One: You will say, "There, there, I'll handle it," hand me
an icy cocktail, and concierge it all for me.

Two: You will murmur, "There, there, you can do it,
you're hella' smart," while handing me freshly sharpened
pencils and Post-its. As well as a cocktail.

Three: Net neutrality. You won't do anything. You'll at
least do no harm.

Four: No help is provided, no support, no cocktail. In fact,
you are actively hazing me for even trying to address my
audit. You're saying: "Fuck 'em! Just throw a shoebox
of receipts at them!" Perhaps subtly implying that I am a
loser for even taking my $34,000 audit seriously—that it
is a sign of my extreme neurosis.

"GODDAMN IT!" I yell at him. I pour his smelly tea all over
the lawn. Professor Moonbeam looks at me with a guarded expression. I am not enlightened, but I do hold the building's title. He must
tread carefully.

I RETURN FROM teaching (otherwise known as "paid employment") at
5 p.m. Three vans are parked in our driveway, their doors flung open,
their contents blasted all over our backyard. There are red prayer books,
golden necklaces, purple scarves, black Hindu lingams everywhere.

They are hammering. And hammering. And hammering. Zing!
Zing! Zing!

Charlie meets me at the back door, apologetic, but also thoughtful, as if he is sharing a very interesting insight about this diligent
group.

"They've never had the space and time to actually empty out and
rebuild the vans. Okay!" he yells to the group, clapping, "day's over!"

Charlie has the sense to immediately mix me an icy cocktail, even though no one else is apparently consuming anything but mung beans, phlegm, and air.

I take a sip and almost miss him saying, "Um, and they need to stay here a few extra days—"

Before I can respond, Shakti is at my side. He bows, offering me a small statue. "It's a Ganesha. Blessed for you. He removes all obstacles."

"See?" Charlie says. "Removes all obstacles."

Shakti says, "Charlie told us about your tax problem. We are praying for you."

"Thank you," I say, once again touched.

And in fact, as the sun goes down and candles are lit, I do feel a bit better. The cocktail helps, as does some medical cannabis Charlie slips me. We all sit down to another curry Charlie has made, along with a smorgasbord of dinged aluminum trays of vegetarian Indian food—peas, potatoes, lentils—from the tour. There seems to be a quiet consensus among the brotherhood that The Girlfriend is about to Flip Out. Everyone is eagerly passing food to me as though I were a fragile bipolar invalid princess.

There's a door knock.

And here they come, the Gentleman Callers. They've come to fraternize with the Hindu monks, of course, but clearly Charlie has also sounded the alarm about my audit.

Which is to say, the Gentlemen Callers enter as solemnly, and cradle their gifts as carefully, as Chinese court eunuchs carrying jars of their private parts.

They, in short, have dug down into their special magical archival mines and brought up . . . their 2015 paper receipts.

"We heard all about your audit," Jerry says, smoothing his Utilikilt.

"Trust me," Bradford whispers, "these are the really good

receipts." He utters that in the same hushed tones as you would say, "Sun Ra on vinyl."

Bradley hands me a shoebox of receipts. The actual shoebox is for some sort of exotic Italian loafer—Ferrante!

Tex proudly hands me his receipts, in a dented manila envelope, puffy with age, as carefully as if this were a raft of winning lottery tickets.

"Laura always does our taxes," Jerry says. "I can only offer you a bottle of her producer's merlot."

"I'm very touched," I admit. "That you all went to this effort." Everyone bows.

"Ganesha provides!"


IN THE MORNING, slightly hungover, I piece through the receipts.

The attention is apparent. They are, indeed, minor works of art, Bradford's in particular. Each receipt is annotated at the bottom in florid penmanship, glorious, sweeping. And, as Bradford lives alone with a cat and never eats out except with opera people, these are all in fact "business expenses."

First problem: THE LEGALITY, as they aren't actually *my* arts-related expenses. Second problem: Bradford neither makes very much nor spends very much.

"$23.44!" he writes fussily.

Charlie has also handed me the crumpled manila envelope that is the crown jewel of his paperwork: his gas receipts. Because we drive together to various meetings, for occasional theater or performance projects, these would, technically, be legal. That's right! Eureka!

We're going to take down this $34,000 elephant $8 (and sometimes as little as $3.62) at a time!

In the heat of summer, there are, of course, now ants, exacerbated by the Indian food and smelly tea and ripening avocados.

But here again, Ganesha. Looking for these Costco ant traps I bought, in the highest shelf in the kitchen, I pull a cupboard open and it all rains down on me. . . .

The holy grail.

Receipts. VISA statements. Canceled checks. All of my date books dating back to 2008. It's the *Da Vinci Code* and I've found the codex! I crow hoarsely with excitement.

I decide I'm going medieval. I'm channeling what Charlie thinks is my latent Asperger's. And I'm okay with it. Bring it on.

The ugly glasses are coming out, the ones from Walgreen's that are my actual real prescription. That's right. The bad boys. The 2.75s. Gone are the days when I thought I could get away with $9.99 glasses that were 2.25s and kind of Tina Fey-looking.

No: the kooky purple ones that make me look like Moms Mabley are the only ones I can actually see with.

I select a piece of super ugly clothing. The BIG Pema Bollywood pants, and a Pokémon GO shirt. And my retired red Crocs.

It's my medieval tax warrior costume.

I assemble around myself my various Hindu trinkets, statuettes, sacred fruit. I go to Office Depot. I decide I will buy the hugest binder I can find—a five-incher. No, I will get two—I am going to do this in duplicate. These binders—jet black and blood red—are so massive they are like jaws of life, or death. These are medieval torture instruments.

I begin to read IRS code like sacred scrolls, the Bhagavad Gita. If husband and wife travel together for work, they can deduct 100 percent of travel for business. But if they make a side trip to Boston by train to visit her sick dad, they cannot deduct that. Even on business, though, they can only deduct half the food.

I buy one thousand page protectors. As in the Hindu mantras, I won't stop until I have filled 880 of them (a magic number). Every gas receipt gets its own sleeve. Every category is color coded.

I cross-link each entry two to three times in mechanical pencil. It becomes my personal Talmud. For every computer entry, there is a check stub, a bank statement, an invoice, and a receipt.

I start to become very excited. It's like a performance art piece. This thing is going to be in New York's MOMA. It is a paper document of extraordinary resonance. It weighs twenty pounds.

Due to the burden of proof it represents, it is a piece of conceptual art worth $34,000.

Spontaneously, the state of California bursts into fires. I wonder whether I should store my binders in a fireproof locker?


IT'S THE NIGHT before my audit. 9:30 p.m.

I'm sitting up in bed with my masterpiece around me. Just as I'm about to triumphantly snap my binders shut, two nagging questions come to me:

1. My "writing office." Is that part of my house or is it listed as a separate deduction? Where does writing take place? Can it take place in two places? Does it exceed 35 percent of my home?!?

2. If I drive more than twenty-five miles across town to a business dinner, is that just mileage or does it go into the category marked "Travel"?

My mind is a snarl of receipts, categories, Excel spreadsheets . . .
("Is there a NOUN you might disturb? Pair it with an ACTION
verb!")

"Jeez," I say, biting my lip, trying to focus, which is difficult as I
appear to hear . . . thumping.

I pad downstairs in disbelief. There are like a dozen Hindu crew
members mingling in our downstairs, male and female. Charlie is
practicing yoga asanas with the men, a couple of Indian women in
saris are frying naan at our stove, and our washing machine, which is
in our kitchen, is going full blazes—thumping, thumping, thumping!

A female crew member named Salma—also in white pajamas—
explains it to me. She has a strong German accent.

"In the woman's house, Leonore had an allergic reaction to the
pillow foam, and was trying to sleep. Since the washing machine
there was near Leonore's bedroom, I wanted to wash Amma's linens
here so Leonore can get some rest."

I pull Charlie aside. "Amma's linens?"

He explains. Because Amma is a holy guru, she must have fresh
linens every day, and there are certain rules about them, like they
need to be facing east or west and need to be sprinkled with lavender
or tamarind—

I freak out.

"Why is your Hindu 'mother' so needy? Where's *my* mother?"

I storm back into the kitchen full of Hindu devotees and scream
into their faces, like Linda Blair in *The Exorcist*: "I'm getting audited
by the IRS for $34,000 and it is my washing machine not your Hindu
mother's and get out of my house or 'home office' or one-quarter home
office or whatever it's called right now. . . . Fuuuuuuukyouuuuuuu!"

THE MORNING OF my audit, my male IRS agent has come down with a mysterious bug. Perhaps it's the same bug that got my old Bear accountants.

A female IRS agent steps in.

I am completely shattered and drained and exhausted.

But it's true that I speak slowly, with lots of pauses, and don't react. "This is the kind of research I do," I explain. "It's all about science and depression and menopause. So much menopause. I am a writer. At times." Upon perusal, we see that Malik simply forgot to log one $20,000 contract payment. You can see all the fluttering tissue 1099s that have a pencil checkmark at the bottom right corner, and then there's one that doesn't.

Clank of the dungeon.

The IRS agent revises the tab down to $4,700. Ganesha!

I'd Rather Be "August" Wilson

# Tampa

I WAS WALKING IN Brookleaf Park this morning. In front of the Kidsplay Children's Museum was a radiant young mom taking iPhone photos of her adorable blonde young son.

*One and a half,* I think. Barely walking, halfway between baby and toddler, when they're only half-formed. They're made of a jellylike substance called Baby. They are almost two-year-olds, but they're still made of Baby.

He was trying to climb onto the red *K* of "Kidsplay." He was picture-perfect in his white-and-blue-striped jumper.

The Kidsplay Museum is in a parklike, rhapsodic glen with a symphony of somewhat rare yet native plants, those certain kinds of important wild grasses. An open amphitheater is fringed by a canopy of willows. Colorful well-kept miniplaygrounds demonstrate the science's deep and intuitive principles: gravity, rotation, flight.

"Hands on! Hands on!" you can hear the Stanford-educated mothers in sunhats calling out, bouncing their BabyBjörns made of hemp(?), Hold Everything Tupperwares of homemade mini banana muffins, and BHP-free water bottles.

I remember, when I was a younger mom, a time of healthy snacks. The idea was, if you cut healthy food (cucumber, cantaloupe) into smiley faces and animal shapes with special fringed cutting tools (dot with raisins for eyes) and place them in your child's cooling pak (mysteriously but pleasingly spelled with a *k*), your child will eat them!

It's such an appealing fantasy, the perfectly constrained/constructed/articulated ballet canvas of motherhood. It invokes child psychology and early education and a deft hand to use the melon baller and a bit of visual artistry to add a dab of color balanced by a calm spirit because one went to morning yoga.

I so miss that idea.

It's like no children who ever set foot into the Kidsplay Museum are obnoxious or smelly or interested in picking their nose. Oh no, with delight they crawl through a rain forest and play with bugs and watch a starfish grow.

Oh, if only I had left my children in there, my daughters. They would still be two and six, in high ponytails, and all would be well. They would still be eating healthy food, delicious, cut up into aardvarks. They would still be in yellow safety helmets driving little cars around the track and tripping through the singing fountains.


WHICH IS TO SAY, I wasn't aware of how long parenting would take. If I'd known, maybe I wouldn't have blown out of the starting blocks so quickly. I wouldn't have played all that Mozart during pregnancy. I wouldn't have pumped all that breast milk and measured it to the half-ounce. I wouldn't have taken my six-month-old babies to learn drumming at Gymboree. When they could barely sit up. Drumming!

I was so proud of getting two girls through childhood without either of them having swallowed a bead. For years I was fixated on that—choking on a bead. I guess the bar was fairly low. No one choked on a bead. I rocked at motherhood!

Now my daughters are tween/teenagers and it's like snakes popping out of a can. Why did I put in so much effort when they were small? I should have rested for ten or twelve years. To be ready for *this*.

Which is to say, unfortunately, instead of resolving itself, somehow, due to the wayward and inconvenient hearts of adolescents, the story of JJ has continued. Remember? JJ? Suicidal fifteen-year-old boy from Tampa?

Over these past several months, since Sally began texting with JJ, there have been many cliff-hangers. All narrated, minute-by-minute, via buzzing texts.

JJ sitting alone under a freeway bridge at night in the rain, watching traffic, not able to go home.

JJ getting into a car with teens he didn't know were drunk.

JJ's Aunt Debra being taken to the hospital in an ambulance, he doesn't know why.

JJ looking into a mirror and cutting himself with glass, blood everywhere.

JJ high on drugs and not making sense.

JJ having a panic attack, spiraling.

The issues appear to be:

His Aunt Debra, who is like a mom to him, has a mysterious illness. He may lose her. Then there would be no reason to live. (Although other threads say Aunt Debra is suffocatingly overprotective.)

When Aunt Debra gets sick, he then has to stay with his

uncle, who hates him. Although there is also the thread
that his uncle and wife insist that he eat meals with their
family, including his cousins, which makes him feel sick.
Both sets of grandparents are homophobic and hate him.
He is messing up at school and disappointing everyone.
  Though he appears to be bright and accelerated and
  takes Java programming classes during the summer.
Also, his antidepressant medication appears sometimes
  working and sometimes not working. When it's not
  working, he wants to give up because he has tried so
  many things and he can't try any more.
Wednesday is the day of the week he sees his doctor. He
  begins cheerful but by 6 p.m. every evening his mood
  starts going down.


But there have been pluses, too.

On good afternoons, Sally sits up on pillows in bed doing her
homework while her little phone vibrates and vibrates. There is comfort. Connection. Laughter. She carries her phone from one room to
another like a pet.

Sally has a bad day at school, and comes home to a package.

JJ has sent Sally this cunning, multifolded gift box he has pains-
takingly hand made. It is painted with rainbows and hearts, with
Sally in the middle, her face rendered in the beautiful, precise hand
of love. There is also self-deprecating humor. There's a card of a unicorn that farts. There are funny cartoons, filled with many tiny JJ
caricatures, cats and Japanese anime characters. Sally is filled with
sunlight.

When calm, JJ has the most extraordinary sense of attention, and
is full of gratefulness, sweetness, hugs.

Sally sends a package back to JJ filled with mysterious beloved objects. A small robot doll she got at the Anime Convention. Striped orange and yellow troll horns she handcrafted out of balsa wood. A magical feather. Notes in a secret language.

It is an ecosystem that Sally maintains, protects, and that, in some sense, emotionally sustains her. I think.

It's just the hours, the punishing hours.

Sometimes in the evening, Sally gets exhausted with JJ's panic attacks. She has homework to do, so she hands her phone to me so I can take over the emergency texting. *This is really*, I think, *not how teen alienation is supposed to work.*

He knows I am Sally's mom, he calls me a "cool mom," and I try to be a calm presence for several coasts. One Wednesday, when JJ's really freaking out, I ask him to draw something for me.

"What?" he types.

"Your cat." He does, and sends it.

"Amazing!" I say.

"It's not," he says.

"I'll show you a cat that's NOT amazing." I draw a bad cat. It's amusing. He laughs. He says he feels better. I still have that cat today. Sally is so grateful I've bought her free time. But within two hours he is down again.

Obviously, these cycles are wearing on us. Sally was anxious about JJ, now I am too. She'll ask me fretfully in the morning if I've heard from JJ. In the afternoon, I'll ask if she has. The good thing is that I'm close with my tween. The bad thing? It feels like we're army medics playing a game of Operation on a tarantula.

I'm at the very least failing my maternal role of Providing Oceanic Calm that quite frankly I wish somebody, anybody, would provide for me.

It always begs the question: "What am I supposed to learn today?"

Sally's new gambit is that she really wants to visit JJ in Tampa. It's her dearest wish. Is that JJ's dearest wish? His text:

**I really really want to meet you guys but I'm afraid when Sally sees me she will hate me.**

Because apparently due to his problematic eyesight he has to wear these really thick glasses. We assume.

Because remember, the only communication has been by text. They've never talked, because teens don't use phones as "phones." Packages of art have been exchanged but no photos—there's no Snapchat or Instagram. Nothing.

"Watch the movie *CATFISH*," Tiger Aunt Kaitlin broods. "*CATFISH*. 'JJ' is likely to be a sixty-two-year-old man or scary obese woman in a trailer. A pedophile."

I TURN, as usual, to my therapist friend Yolanda.

"First question," she says. "You have to ask yourself. Seriously. Is your ego getting massaged by communicating with JJ and being such a 'cool' mom?"

"Honestly," I say, "maybe it felt like that for a moment, like that time we drew cats. But mostly his situation is too vast and complicated and unsolvable, and I fail as much as I succeed. I feel powerless and like I'm failing as a mother because I can't protect my daughter from sadness. So no, it doesn't feel very flattering."

"Fair enough. It's interesting. Sally is what, eleven, right?"

"Just turned twelve."

"Uh-huh. In my practice, there are a number of teen girls with suicidal gay male teen friends. It's a common trope."

"What's that about?" I'm grateful that at least Yolanda is considering that JJ might be a real person, rather than a sixty-two-year-old CATFISH.

"These girls are experiencing huge emotions within themselves, which can be overwhelming. Dealing with the drama of their gay male teen friends is a way to play out those feelings, but on another canvas."

"So, Sally—?"

"She may be feeling unstable inside, but instead of telling her parents, she helps JJ with JJ's drama. It may give her a sense a control, worth, agency."

The conclusion: we have a mess on our hands. Sally should get therapy.

I should get therapy.

Sally and JJ can communicate, but I am to let go entirely. I am to cut off all communication with JJ. I am violating boundaries, muddying waters.

I need to be the mother, the parent, and keep my distance.


I INFORM SALLY of the prognosis.

"Are you depressed, honey?" I ask. "Do you feel unstable?" But asking that of a teen is like asking a *top* if it feels unstable.

Sally denies being depressed, says she doesn't want to go to therapy, and insists all she wants is to go to Tampa to meet JJ.

"Are you sure JJ wants us to come?" I ask.

"Of course!"

"Didn't you say he can't even predict where he'll be in summer?"

"He'll be there," she says with a calm I myself do not have, "he'll be there."

. . .

So of course, IN VIOLATION OF EVERYTHING THERAPIST
YOLANDA SAID!!! I book a trip to Tampa. Because Sally is asking
me over and over and over. She does not vary here. Her requests are
constant. And I don't have sense. But I do have air miles.

We triangulate a week in early August. The story I tell myself
is that we are going to Tampa to Have Fun! Never mind that, even
after I've booked flights and a hotel, JJ can't say where he'll be. At
his aunts'. Uncle's. Grandparents'. I cling to the fact that we at least
have a home address for Aunt Jill (and presumably Aunt Debra), in
an apartment complex that snail mail has at least successfully come
from and has been delivered to. I have google-imaged this address—
the blurry photo reveals a small unit whose cheerful front porch
features two blue folding chairs and several potted plants. We can at
least drive by there, as you would by the home of Elvis in Graceland.
Hopefully, Sally will get to meet JJ, somehow (for lunch, dinner?
Marie Callender's?) . . . but if not, she and I will drive seventy-seven
miles to Orlando to Walt Disney World!

Two weeks out, Sally asks, quietly, "If we go to Tampa and JJ is
dead, can we at least visit his gravesite?"

"Yes," I say, completely saddened, though I decide to lunge for
the next parental ring. "But JJ will be alive! I guarantee you!"

One week before our trip, the mood lightens. JJ and Sally are
making happy plans, of watching movies together and making pillow
forts and meeting his cats. But come Saturday, Aunt Debra suddenly
takes mysteriously ill. JJ is moved to his uncle's house, where he is a
house prisoner. His uncle is a jailer.

Even I am starting to lose my patience now. (As Kaitlin would
say: "Is that the telltale smell of . . . CATFISH?") I say to Sally,
"Look. Doesn't it seem like a coincidence that JJ is 'moved to his

uncle's house' the exact week we're coming? If JJ doesn't want to meet us, really, there's nothing we can do."

"I'm meeting JJ," Sally repeats, with an eerie belief. "I can't wait to meet JJ."

I am the worst mother ever.


I HATE FLYING, and Florida's Gulf Coast winds are superbumpy. I grip my armrests, nauseated.

The prognosis for a horrible outcome is 90 percent certain.

It's as if I myself am a suicide bomber who has pointed the nose of the plane toward disaster.

Worst of all is the excitement Sally is clearly feeling, that she is going to meet JJ! Looking out the window at the storm clouds, her face is radiant with joy.

I pat her dry hand with my sweaty one and repeat the mantra that's less for her than for me: "At the very least, we can drive by his aunts' house tomorrow. At the very least, there will be evidence she exists, or her car exists, or something."

We touch down in Tampa. We see ads for Disney World, the happiest place on earth. It's pouring rain.

We drift down the escalator, past multiple WELCOME TO TAMPA! signs. "At the very least, we can drive to Disney World!" I say. "We're going to have fun!"

"Yes, we are!" Sally agrees, all smiles.

We wait in the rental car line. The passengers and tourists around us, with Bermuda shirts and beach gear, look so hopeful. Otherwise known as lost and out of place. We are all fools. Total fools. In a tropical downpour.

I try not to look over at Sally. My expectation is, now that we have landed, the texts will mysteriously stop. And in fact, Sally is sitting on a couch with her backpack, looking peaceful, but her phone is also not buzzing.

"Disney World!" I exclaim heartily. "This will be fun."

It is in the car, driving through a tropical storm, past less-than-reassuring Florida tourism billboards—ZIPLINE OVER GATORS!—when suddenly Sally pipes up. "Oh good. Aunt Debra is better. So Aunt Jill is coming to pick him up from his uncle's."

So we're "on" again. Theoretically.

All of a sudden, JJ wants to know if he can come over—okay!—and what time will we be at our place. We throw out 5 p.m. as a number.

Now that this is supposedly moving forward, my stomach is starting to churn. There is, all at once, the hope that he will show up, the dread that he won't, and the worry that he will show up and it will be not who we expect and I will have to call the Florida police (but what sort of person would pull a ruse like this on a twelve-year-old girl and her fifty-six-year-old mother?).

We check into our lake cottage. It is a slightly mildewy vacation home with kayaks waiting, a vegetable garden, and a small hot tub. We have no idea where we are in relation to town. We're starving.

"We have time," I say. "Let's go to that Mexican place on the corner."


WE DO, and order a couple of burritos . . . but the service at this sleepy restaurant is weirdly slow.

The clocks ticks to 4:45.

"We have to get it to go. No time."

"Okay," Sally says.

I'm suddenly in a panic, throwing money at them as we grab searing hot Styrofoam containers. I feel like nothing can be left to chance. JJ is a mirage that will blow away at any second. Everything about this has a fatalistic Anna Karenina feeling about it. JJ and Aunt Jill come to the house, we miss them by five minutes, then his grandparents fly him to Cuba with the wrong medication—

One thing is clear: If I am ever to see this vibrating fictional creature, I will slam an iron ankle bracelet on him.

Now we speed bumpily back home. In the rain. Sally gazes out the window at Florida, quietly ecstatic. I just continue to see rain.

We scream in at 4:57. We lay our Styrofoam boxes around the high glass table. Five o'clock comes.

Nothing.

5:15. Nothing.

It has stopped raining, anyway.

A cloudy, murky, silvery mist persists.

Sally eats her burrito contentedly. Her excitement is pure and continuous. Her phone buzzes. JJ and Aunt Jill are setting off a little later than they thought, and, what with traffic, will be another thirty minutes.

6 p.m. comes.

The phone buzzes. JJ reports—ten minutes away.

6:15 comes.

6:20.

At 6:28 I think I hear a sound from the street. I peer out the curtains. A small blue sedan appears to be pulling up to the curb.

In one motion, Sally rises from the table, flings open the front door and starts running, the wind at her back, the way you would run toward a whaling ship that has just come home after a seven-year journey.

And through a pane of mildewy glass, I do in fact see two figures. A heavyset fortysomething woman with a blonde pageboy haircut and a small boy with dyed green hair and indeed large owl-like—

though not un-cute—black glasses. He is in a purple cape, and orange and yellow troll horns.

"Oh my God!" I exclaim. "JJ! He's in cosplay!"

Sally and JJ run toward each other and hug. In truth, she is so tall for her age, she lifts him up into the air.

Like a cat.

Because you know what? Apparently: "Cats understand."

For a blissful, surreal week in Tampa, there is no fighting, sulking, nor any rip in the cosmic fabric. It is like two atomic particles that, when separated, created these electric sparks and darkness via buzzing phones. But upon falling gravitationally together, they are in a steady state. They live together, finally, undisturbed, watch cartoons, draw pictures, eat tomato soup, in a magical pillow fort of their own making.

Okay, so, let me say this. In the long run, transitioning out of tweenhood, this will not last forever. Life is, as we say, complicated.

You have questions—as I did. What was going on with JJ's Aunt Debra? Something about "better medication," he said, that she was "better." (Perhaps JJ's antidepressant medication, which his doctors kept changing on him, was better?) His Aunt Jill was cordial during the week, if busy with work and her sister's doctor's appointments, so happy to have some child care. Why all those crazy texts, about all those dire situations? "Sometimes I panic," JJ says. "I'm sorry." We see no cuts on him. Does he make things up? How much of any of this was true? Some answers came, some didn't.

But let us leave that aside in today's storytelling. In that one moment . . .

As they ran toward each other in the mist . . .

It was like experiencing something totally pure. It made no sense.

It was very beautiful.

The fact is that he did exist—and in the moment it was enough. Because very occasionally, when you least expect it, Love Wins.

# "Fall" into "September"/"October"/ "November"/"December

# Marriage in the Middle Ages

## I Do or I Don't?

O F COURSE, AS PURE—if unlikely—as teen love is, in middle age, cohabiting? It's hard for pure love to be pure, or love, or, sometimes, anything but intense, deep irritation.

Which is to say, since the Hindu monks left, things have been rocky with Charlie and me, to say the least.

He has been unemployed for two months. The VW needs a new headlight.

He is reading food blogs for—what?—how many hours a day?

I am working like a dog on a colleague's manuscript edit—tedious and not inspiring, but it will pay.

The house is a wreck.

Maybe Charlie can bring in a little income so Luz can come more often?

I say, "Even a thousand dollars a month?"

"What do you expect me to do?" he scoffs. "Bag groceries at Trader Joe's?"

I shrug and say, "Well . . ." It seems like that's a thing artisanally employed creative people our age are doing. With the proper perspective, working at Trader Joe's could be viewed as a kind of party: the festive Hawaiian shirts, the deep discounts on products that are soy and gluten-free, in Pasadena perhaps one could even bike there, get some of that good cardio!

But astonishingly, the capper is that Charlie and I had the most royal fight.

It was so stupid.

Which is to say, recently, we've been having all these tiring fights in the kitchen, about:

Socialism

Single-payer health care

How everything is better in Denmark. So many of his
      sentences start "But in Denmark . . . "

"Where the income tax rate is 70 percent!" I yell.

The other night, he raged: "If you can point out to me how the current Supreme Court actually reflects the will of the people? I'm moving to Mexico."

Meaning that if building the wall and straight wedding cakes actually reflect the popular vote—"the *popular* one!"—he can no longer tolerate living in the United States.

"You're moving to Mexico?" I erupted. "Because you don't like the composition of our Supreme Court? Hashtag Second World Problems!"

"I am," he blazed. "I'm moving to Mexico."

"The Mexicans are really going to welcome you with open arms. You're the freelance theater producer they've been looking for. That's why they keep crossing the border north, trying to find you. You don't even speak Spanish, for God's sake!"

I screamed: "WHY AM I THE ONE IN THIS HOUSE WHO HAS TO USE LOGIC???"

"I JUST DON'T THINK I can do it anymore," I say to Marilyn and her husband Barry. We always have a nice barter system going. I've driven to their lovely canyon home to lend them some movie screeners, in exchange for the loan of an extra printer for use by my daughters. And also a huge bag of lemons from their tree.

"What do you mean 'it'?" Marilyn asks.

"I think Charlie may just be too eccentric!" I exclaim. "With the Hinduism and the beads and the cannabis and the poverty and his breaking-down VW, which he calls 'Button.'" I shudder in horror. "He has a name for his car."

"I'm eccentric!" Barry parries, putting down a platter of tuna fish and chips and cut-up apples and cheese.

"His astronomy thing!" Marilyn exclaims. It's true: Barry's passion for amateur astronomy can stretch to fifteen hours a week. Sometimes short desert trips are involved.

"I know, Barry," I say. "But you do things around the house and you have health insurance and you're officially retired from that . . . legal stuff you used to do. . . ."

"Patents," he says.

"I mean, you guys are like us, but the better, fifteen-years-older version. It's like you guys caught the growth of the baby boom, and we caught the tail. It's like I'm not quite old enough, with my still school-aged girls, and nor am I quite wealthy enough, to be pulling off the 'fun Second Husband' thing. Marilyn, you began as an actress, right?"

"Yes!" she exclaims, shaking out her grayish but still-full ringlets. "I traveled to England, went to Oxford, did all the Shakespeare. . . ."

"But then you went into business consulting and you invented all those team-building workshops and made a zillion dollars!" I say.

"I was lucky," she demurs. "There was some good timing."

"So you have the underground continent of money—that subterranean foundation—so that you can be this seemingly quirky boomer couple, with all your wacky hobbies, and all your—what—Tibetan drum circles, and your sugar cleanses, but it's not like the bone is rubbing against bone or joint against joint." I bring my hands together in a crushing motion. "I mean, look at your house, it's gigantic!"

"Your house is big, too," Marilyn declares.

"It is, but it's wooden, and the sound! It's like living inside an acoustic guitar! Every noise resonates!"

"It is true that this home is a blessing," Marilyn admits.

"Separate bedrooms!" Barry adds, eyebrows raised.

"He snores," Marilyn says.

"Not that I'm aware of," he says.

"How would you know?" she asks.

"Ah well," he says, pouring prosecco.

"Oh sweetie," she says, sitting next to him and putting her arm around him. "It's not that we can't visit each other when we feel like it."

"'Tis true," he says, "and I can watch my World War II documentaries. And sports!"

"It's so wonderful not to watch sports!" she exclaims. "But the point is, we still love each other. Other couples our age—late sixties? You can see the deadness in their eyes, but as my friend Gemma told me, about herself and her husband, 'We're 'beyond divorce.' "

"Meaning?"

"There was a moment when they *could* have gotten divorced, when both kids left for college, but they didn't get it together in time. Now that door has closed, they're just both too lazy. . . . Why divorce when you're turning seventy? But Gemma has put an earth-positive spin on it—'like beyond meat,' she says, 'it's 'beyond divorce.'"

"My aunt divorced my uncle when she was eighty!" Barry exclaims. "She said, 'I have ten years left! Why should I spend it with this lump?' She started painting and went to Europe—she has been having a grand old time!"

"But you love Charlie," Marilyn says. "I remember when you both first got together. What a romance! He's your soul mate!"

"Well, he may be my soul mate—you know, the person who is like a mirror? But I've looked in the mirror and I haven't always liked what I've seen. Screaming 'fuck you!' at those poor Hindu monks. Though that was justified."

"But at heart, you do love him."

"Could you see ever getting married to him?" Barry asks.

"Weddings are fun!" Marilyn exclaims, as they snuggle around cheese.

"At this point, if we did get married," I say, "it would solely be for health insurance purposes. I'm not even convinced I wish marriage on my own daughters!" I suddenly realize. "The thought of Hannah walking down the aisle with some twentysomething guy. . . . Are we 'giving her away'? Into what? Never mind romantic love, what they're actually doing is signing a legal contract to meld their finances. What if he's charming on the surface, but bad with money? What are the chances this young yokel is going to have more sound financial habits than the entire clan of Loh, which, by the way, is headed by the dragon lady, my incredibly responsible sister, who could run a small country? And provide everyone excellent and affordable health insurance, btw?"

"Ah yes, the Loh family!" Marilyn exclaims. "It's a very Asian thing," she adds, to Barry.

"Right, you've told me," he says. "Where family interest rates are set . . ."

"In the 1990s it was 6 percent. Six percent!" I exclaim. "Now it's closer to 3. But more deeply than that, I worry that I'm just too irritable to live with a man anymore. At least in the shared space we have. Let me tell you the story of my friend Karen—she's about my age, fifty-four, divorced, two sons off in college. Karen met Leo in her apartment building on Melrose. Leo is a menschy and wonderful—and gainfully employed—film editor guy. He lives two floors down. It has been ideal. He rises early, she is an insomniac. . . ."

"Like us," Marilyn adds.

"I mean, sometimes I really want Charlie in bed with me. I need that electrical grounding, that *Waiting to Exhale* thing, that soft place to fall where you spoon him or he spoons you."

"But sometimes the angle isn't quite right, there is snoring, and, man, if you get a good bed pillow!" Marilyn exclaims.

"And she wants the temperature so cold," Barry adds, "like a tomb."

"And have you heard of these fabulous new weighted blankets?" Marilyn asks. "They're good for anxiety."

"Anyway, for Karen, if she has a spider or something, Leo can come right over. But of course, two apartments are expensive. They could save money by moving in together. To, let's say, this adorable Spanish-style bungalow Karen and I found online. Three bedrooms, two baths, converted garage. Plenty of room for everyone to have their own space.

"So we're walking through this bungalow, and it's cute," I continue. "I hear myself chiming in with my usual responses: 'You could have a kitchen herb garden! This fire pit is perfect for entertaining! Here's the den where you can binge watch your shows together!' But it was like dealing with an alien. Karen just wasn't getting excited about, well, moving in, and nesting. She had already done that with a husband and two sons, both in college. She's looking at this homey kitchen with its cheerful skylights and her only comment is 'Oh boy, I'd have to share a fridge again.' It was like walking through a cheerful IKEA display of the bedroom of a college student. Cute, but from a former life.

"And afterward, we go to a coffee bar and she says, 'Leo is a great, great guy. But his taste in music is awful! It's this streaming that's a constant sort of house music jushjushjush, from his tablet, awful fidelity, leaves it on when he's not even in the room. It's noise pollution.'

"And I say: 'Well, that could be solved with headphones! You love each other!' But even as I'm saying that, I'm thinking, *Egad. Charlie's Hindu trance music drives me nuts and I am growing increasingly allergic to the aroma of his smelly incense! It's like having soap shoved into your mouth!*"

"Really?" Barry exclaims. "I like the smell of incense."

"I don't know if it's because I'm menopausal," I say, "but so many things irritate me now. Sounds! Smells! His clothing and laundry, piled on our bench in the bedroom!"

"Actually I'm the one who does that," says Marilyn. "I'm the messy one."

"But she has her own bedroom!" Barry exclaims.

"And Leo has these two dogs that Karen finds too 'lungey.' . . . And suddenly it sounds sensible to not move into the cute Spanish-style house, and Karen and I realize there may be a word for us. Instead of 'postdivorce,' maybe we're both 'postcohab,' or 'postcohabitation'? Maybe we just can't do it anymore!"

"Are you saying you're against marriage?" Barry asks.

"Do you regret marrying Ben?" Marilyn asks.

"Well no," I say. "Looking back, I realize marriage isn't the culprit, in the same way a fancy school versus a state school isn't really the culprit—you may well get a decent education from each. I married the right man at the right time, and made the right kids. Ben is the type of man you actually do marry. He saves money and fixes things and is an ocean of sanity. I was filing some papers recently and realized I still have an old Writer's Guild Death and Dismemberment policy. That's what I told my daughters, 'It's not just death. It has to be dismemberment. So make sure, in the flaming train wreck, you cut off at least part of one of my fingers.' "

"Ghoulish!" says Barry.

"The benefactor was still my ex-husband Ben, and upon thinking about it I decided to leave it that way. That $20,000 would be safest with him. He'd invest it conservatively for our girls. Charlie would blow half of it on Hindu prosperity candles. That's really the way I feel! Marriage was just the name of a set of ideas we had, then."

"I remember your wedding," Marilyn says. "It was fun!"

"I remember initially feeling that 'marriage' sounded so conventional, and I didn't want to be a 'wife.' I told Ben—upon buying our second house together, right?—we should have a 'commitment ceremony.' And he said, 'My mom is not flying in from Minnesota for a commitment ceremony!'

"So we did throw a wedding and I did buy a gown and this fancy stylist did my hair in this awful too-ornate way, making me late to my own wedding. We got married fairly straightforwardly by a Lutheran minister friend, even though it was 104 degrees that day, margaritas were being served, the bartender got drunk, and one of our guests (my boss) was rushed to the emergency room. My husband's hip musician colleagues refused to play 'Mustang Sally,' which was my one request. But then Chick Corea—whom Ben was working with at the time, true story—Chick Corea made a surprise late arrival, he vamped on 'All Blues,' everyone joined, and I'm told I led sixteen women in a drunken ballet. My wonderful choreographer friend Raiford was there. I do remember him saying, as we careened all over our cramped Van Nuys deck, fringed with tea lights: 'Think very Egyptian, ladies. Less is more, less is more.'

"So marriage was something we decided to call it at that time, to rally our friends and families to us. And, in the years to come, when as fate dictates, not everyone stays around, no regrets over the memories. And oh, the platters. There were some really beautiful platters."

"That is true," Marilyn says, grasping Barry's hand. "The kitchenware of weddings is very beautiful!"

# The Fantasy of Living Alone

A<small>N EDITOR AT</small> *New York* magazine calls me up with an essay assignment: Living Alone After Fifty. As he writes: "Statistically, these are boom times for middle-aged people who are living alone. Their numbers have nearly doubled since 1999, rising from 13 percent to 21 percent of the 55- to 64-year-old population. Over 50 percent of people 50 or over are single."

T<small>HE TIMING IS PERFECT.</small> I am intrigued both on behalf of the project and on behalf of myself.

I begin working on my magazine assignment, e-mailing all my middle-aged girlfriends who are living alone. My editor, in his thirties, is interested in the fear and despair of fifty-pluses living alone. But horribly for me, to the last woman, they are all thrilled, thrilled, thrilled! to be single!

Danielle, for instance, is having a housewarming party. Flush with her inheritance from her dad, she has bought herself a Silver Lake duplex.

"Oh my God," our gaggle of some dozen women exclaim, as we sip chilled basil-cucumber martinis while getting the tour.

Danielle's freshly redone skylit bachelorette aerie is a calming sea of white warmed with dots of Mediterranean color via fresh flowers, art, and pillows. (Downstairs is a private studio that rents on Airbnb for two thousand dollars a week.) There are cunning natural wood built-ins and frosted glass cabinets that encase any errant clutter in camouflaging ice. None of the herbs in her jewel-box garden window are dead, dying, or brown.

Everything visible is beautiful.

It's like a boutique hotel I want to check into immediately.

"It took a lot of work to get it here," Danielle says. "We had to practically gut the place to get the flow."

"We" includes herself and her dream contractor/sometime actor John Kennedy. "Isn't that funny? My handyman's name is literally John Kennedy."

Danielle swings open the red door to her home office.

"Oh my God!" I exclaim. "It is so exactly like how I'd want my home office to be!"

Here is a creative sanctuary of glowing track lighting, a blonde wood desk, custom-fit bookshelves that—I can see, looking closer—have only classics on them. Unlike me, Danielle has culled her books. Just perusing her quality personal library (and it's *alphabetized*—Cheever! Didion! Eggers!) feels like coming home to a better self.

My own boxy house is defined by large square public rooms, ideal for Quaker meetings or Lutheran potlucks. For all its square footage, I do not have an office. I type from my unmade bed. Collapsing bookshelves on my right are choked with food magazines, PC computer manuals, *ONLINE INVESTING FOR DUMMIES* (none of it mine!). Along the opposite wall is a ragged skyline of Charlie's *New York Times*es and half-read *New Yorker*s.

And, of course, in every corner, there are collapsing piles of Writer's Guild Award screeners. I haven't had a Writer's Guild contract in years, but I can vote on Writer's Guild Awards. Actual working screenwriters are always desperate for my approbation!

All the women moan at Danielle's spa-like master bathroom (fluffy white towels, eucalyptus soaps, flickering aromatherapy candles).

"My house could never be like this," exclaims Irene, a nonprofit administrator, with surprising vehemence, "because if you open any closet in my house, an avalanche of crap will spill out!"

Julia agrees. "My husband Bill? He must have twenty-five, thirty guitars. And amps. And old *Guitar Player* magazines. And these Rubbermaid bins full of power cords. We haven't been able to open the basement door in years."

"You're married to a musician?" Irene asks.

Eyebrows raise, for a horrified beat, to utter the obvious: "No!"

"My forty-seven-year-old husband collects baseball cards," Irene says. "He has 150 boxes of them in the garage. Quasi-hoarding—it's a real issue at our age."

"Right," says Julia. "In our twenties, we had one swing-arm lamp and two milk crates. By now, we've accumulated so much of what George Carlin used to call my 'stuff' and his 'shit'—it's like maintaining an extra ghost person."

Out on Danielle's immaculate teak back deck, I hold up my phone: "Okay, ladies. Here's a *HuffPo* article called 'The Lifestyle More Older Women Are Starting to Embrace.' It says: 'Midlife women are doing it again. As we did in our 20s, we are questioning fundamentals, challenging the status quo, being stubbornly bohemian and embracing the unconventional.' Living alone, for or against?"

"For!" says a lawyer named Serena. "I've lived alone my whole life, in four different countries. What's the big deal? I have my own business, fly a plane, and am so used to managing on my own I'm unworried about the future. Often couples enable each other to become weaker. Instead of two people, you have one and a half people. They just enable each other's bad habits."

"That's true," I say. "When my girls are away, many nights Charlie and I drink red wine, smoke pot, and fall asleep in front of the TV. I'll wake up in the morning in a sea of Kettle Chip crumbs—'Oh honey, no, did we eat that whole bag?' Opening my e-mail, I see iTunes is claiming someone named 'Sandra Loh' bought the *Lord of the Rings* trilogy at midnight for $19.95, a trilogy I already own. Sure, it was fun at the time, but I am a loser. Shit!"

"Oh, since divorcing?" says Andie. "One of the best things? Traveling alone."

"Yes!" says Irene. "The older I get, the more I adore traveling alone, wandering, sketching, eating all the baked goods I want. My husband Luke had a medical conference in Germany, so I flew with him there, then went on to Paris. He calls me and says, 'Good news! We finished early! I can join you!' And the sentence that immediately comes to my mind is 'There is no "U" in Paris.' "

We all laugh and clink our martinis.

"Charlie and I were actually able to get to Paris in connection with a travel magazine piece I got assigned," I now remember. "It seemed it would be so, so romantic. I got a guidebook and lovingly circled the Louvre, Arc de Triomphe, Versailles. . . . Upon arrival, I learned that Charlie had no intention of going to any of these places because they were, quote unquote, 'touristy.' "

"Oh no!" comes the chorus. "So what did you do?"

"Once there, I realized what Charlie liked to do was to sit in cafés in Le Marais reading the *New York Times* and smoking cigarette after cigarette. Why? 'Because everyone smokes in Paris,' he said. He smoked at the window of our hotel room. He smoked during meals, literally at the table, blowing smoke across my steak frites.

He smoked in cabs so much at one point our—mind you, *French*—
cab driver turned around in indignation and . . . guess what? *Irately
ordered him—in English—to stop smoking.*"

As we begin to eat our tasty Thai food (seamlessly delivered), Danielle describes this guy she met a few months earlier on Match.com. "He
spent a weekend here, then never left. He was nice enough—funny, cute,
smart. . . . He initially said he was a 'producer,' but as I've learned, over
the age of forty in Los Angeles, 'producer' is a synonym for 'homeless.'

"The last straw was the hardwood floors. When I told Sean the
refinishers were coming, he complained that now he has to get his
magazines off the floor and he didn't feel like doing that this weekend. To which I said: 'Either this stuff goes or you do. They're coming
Monday, move your shit.'

"So now I'm doing the math. I'm calculating the price, literal and
metaphorical, of a man."

Danielle ticks it off on her fingers. "His income? I don't need. The
sex? It was okay, but you can date and get that—I've been seeing this
guy recently I met on OkCupid and arguably it's better. The ability
to fix things is a plus, but Sean was completely inept and I have John
Kennedy. I do like to watch TV at night, but Sean would talk all
through *Downton Abbey*."

"Did you tell me he used to cook a lot?" asks Julia.

"Yes! But for Sean, it was such a project! It took the whole day!
Who needs that when you can Yelp anything you want, no dishes?"

"That's just like Charlie!" I say. "The cooking projects! First
comes an hour of Talmudic study of the *New York Times* food section. Next is a trip to the farmer's market to buy exotic vegetables,
some of which he may cook for dinner, possibly grilling them, in
some fussy experimental manner. In the process, the kitchen sink fills
with pots, pans, a colander, a mandoline, both a large and a small
food processor, dinosaur-sized tongs."

"Oh, the important kitchen gadgets!" Danielle exclaims. "It's such a male thing! The maestro is in! Hopefully a housecleaning crew will follow!"

"Right!" cries out Julia. "What's with that 'food scientist' guy Alton Brown? He's always cooking, alone, in his kitchen, sterile as the inside of a Patek Philippe watch. The phone doesn't ring, dogs don't run through, children don't howl. He never has to run back to Ralphs for that one thing. He never washes a dish. Whose life is like that? I humbly ask: Aren't there patches of time, while waiting for pasta to boil, when Mr. Brown could rinse off some pots? Transfer a load of socks to the dryer?"

"Exactly," I say. "Men have taken one aspect of housework—cooking—and lifted it to an arcane, time-consuming sport like fly fishing. James Beard has a recipe to make 'perfect scrambled eggs' that requires stirring them for thirty minutes. Meanwhile, for centuries women have been doing all the cooking, and also most of the grocery shopping, housecleaning, laundry, child care, and, oh yeah, the dishes! Forget the Food Channel. When will we get a glamorous Housecleaning Channel, or Laundry Channel? Think of it: a channel of just men in stylish Warby Parker rims artisanally doing laundry!"

"My Midwestern mother-in-law has a cookbook called *The Lutheran Mother's Cookbook*," says Irene. "There are recipes with names like 'Lazy Woman's Pickles' and 'Washday Soup.' This is essentially boiling water that you throw ground beef into, because, you know what? It's wash day."

"And all those f-ing male food writers," Julia says. "Sam Sifton, Michael Pollan. 'Slow Food.' Fuck you. How dare you lecture me about spending more time cooking?"

"You know what we should write?" I say, getting a brainstorm. " 'The Angry Divorced Working Mother's Cookbook.' Between the girls' schedules and mine, I'm in the car twenty hours a week."

"So until car dashboards come with stoves, or trunks with crockpots," says Julia, "no Slow Food movement for us."

I say, "My 'broken family' recipes include Festival of Toast. The Loaded Biscuit. Quesadilla Surprise. Broccoli from Hell—"

"What's that?" everyone wants to know.

"Throw broccoli on a baking sheet, shake on olive oil and salt, and shove it into the oven at 475 for twenty minutes until it's blackened. I discovered it by accident—"

"Here's another recipe," Irene says. " 'How to Roast a Chicken.' Begin by taking the plastic off. Preferably. You should probably take the giblet things out, too, although, to be honest I can't swear I've done that *every* single time and my family is still alive. Then put it into the oven at 350 for two hours."

"Better yet," Serena says, "just pick a roasted chicken up at the store. Sometimes your best cooking utensils are your car keys."

"We just know more who we are now," says Danielle. "In our twenties, we were still forming, as young women. We didn't really know what we wanted. Now we do—"

"Postcohab," I murmur. "Postcohab."


I VISIT MY FRIEND Andy, fifty-two, longtime former writer for an alternative weekly. It stayed weekly but gradually became less alternative. He has been single for over a decade now. In contrast to "A Room of Her Own," Andy has gaily dubbed his 250-square-foot converted garage "The Palace of Failure."

Handing me an espresso, he gives a tour. The Palace of Failure is like a small houseboat, packed with favorite books, DVDs, appliances. To the right are large monitors (TV and computer, flickering), in the middle is an unmade futon topped with wrinkled laundry and sleeping bag that appears to be breathing. To the left is a narrow landing strip of kitchen. It features a "tabletop convection oven" (big enough to bake pizza but not chicken) and ten-gallon water heater ("I can wash dishes or shower but not both").

What's breathing under the sleeping bag turns out to be Andy's nineteen-year-old cat Mingus. Andy picks little pieces of fur off Mingus's back and flicks them onto the rug.

"I'll vacuum it tonight," he says, "or maybe tomorrow." The problem is, to get to the vacuum he has to open the closet door, blocked by his Casio Syndrums.

The rent strikes me as surprisingly high—$945 a month. Andy agrees. "But I don't want to move Mingus. Moves disorient Mingus. Mingus deserves better."

It strikes me that instead of the cat lady, we are in the era of the cat gentleman. "In nineteen years, we've been apart twenty, maybe thirty nights," Andy reports.

His phone dings. He picks it up. "Snorlax!"

"Oh my God," I say. "You play Pokémon GO, too!"

I can't resist. I excitedly pick up my phone—and we spend the next three minutes catching the virtual Snorlax that has appeared in Andy's virtual Palace.

At which point I see it: his pile of *New York Times* crosswords. Hm. Andy and I have more in common than I might have guessed. Which begs the question: Single, would I be Danielle or Andy?

It's the Scared Straight of Singledom.


I DRIVE HOME around 5 p.m., pull into the driveway.

Charlie is sitting in the rocking chair on the porch, as though waiting for a homecoming sailor. He rises, his hand shading his eyes, as he looks searchingly into my face. He is wondering what my wayward mood is.

I'm tired. I've been a little spooked by Andy's place. I know Charlie will enjoy hearing about it—the layout, the contents of the fridge, what *kind* of Syndrums? At thinking about the Snorlax, I can't help cracking into a rueful smile.

We look into each other's faces. He smiles, in his rakish, devil-may-care way. "Oh look," he says, throwing his arms out, "it's the return of Awesome Boyfriend!"

"Oh yeah?" I ask.

"Well, after my triumphant return from Mexico, where I started a small theater troupe doing English translations of Afrofuturist poetry—"

"And puppetry," I add. "Don't forget the puppetry."

"Oh, did you see my viral Snapchat story?" he asks casually. (Note: Charlie is on no social media at all, and never will be.)

"I gave thirty-seven dollars to your GoFundMe. The one from Spain. It was very moving."

He pours us—or rather spigots us—some box red wine.

"Oh my God, the splatter," I say. "But I love the pirate theme."

"It's new, at Von's." He swirls his glass vigorously. "You have to aerate it."

"Should we take it into the yard?" I ask. "Run it around the block?"

And without further comment, we plop into our armchairs on the back porch. He puts out his customary small fussy bowls of nuts. They are Costco nuts in surfboard-shaped bowls and they are probably as tasty as those more wealthy WASPS have put out, over the decades, which perhaps is not saying much, but it's saying something.

And, being for the moment, neither beyond divorce nor postcohab, I realize we do share a love. . . . But what is it?

It is less husband and wife. . . . He is certainly not like a "husband," exactly, whom I cannot expect to "take care" of me. . . . And I am no "wife.". . .

Nor either "boyfriend" and "girlfriend" . . . surely ridiculous terms, at this age? But we are friends, we are family, we are homemates. . . . We gravitate here to our customary formation and quadrants, as night falls. Our rhythm begins again, the glass(es) of wine, the nuts, the conversation.

Perhaps he's my personal clown. I'll research insurance rates on that in the morning.

# Ch-Ch-Ch-Changes

## The Hip

I'VE BEEN DRIVING the girls to school and back on a 6 a.m. to 7 p.m. schedule. To conserve my energy in the middle of the day, I've been going back to bed. I type on my laptop in bed.

I talk on the phone in bed. I eat in bed.

I fantasize about a car shaped like a bed.

One afternoon, I swing my legs right to get out of bed, my hip spasms, and I literally tumble to the floor with a crash.

Charlie has been down at his desk, doing what would previously have been a very un-Charlie thing: researching water heaters. After another blowout that neither of us could endure, he has dug deep within his mantric self and has been learning how to interface with my Second Husband, Angie. He is finding his own kind of Hindu system within her List.

Charlie dashes upstairs. "Honey, are you all right?" He helps me up off the ground and back on to the bed, lightly dusting me off.

"Oh my God," I say. "This is literally the moment the elderly person takes a fall in their New York City apartment and are only found ten days later, their body half-eaten by wolves."

He puts his hands on my shoulders.

"You're not in New York City, and you're not going to be eaten by wolves. Bedbugs, maybe. No! I'm calling your chiropractor."

"Oh no!" I wail. "With this insurance I have? The copayment—"

"Shh," he says. "You're hurting. They can take you at three. I'll drive you."

Charlie could use an adjustment himself, so once again, it's one of those romantic, middle-aged, dual-overdue-doctor's-appointments "dates."

My chiropractor is, in fact, a great first person to visit. She is unfailingly gentle, supportive, positive. I figure her stretching me will function as a kind of exercise. But no, even she says, "You need to start walking a few minutes a day. Park that car just a bit farther out in the lot. Move."

But my hip is popped out. It is painful to walk.

So I decide to rejoin the gym and do Tuesday "gentle yoga." I remembered that it's taught by a lovely sad young woman named Shambhala. It's lying down, stretching, breathing, basically hugging a pillow to soothing tabla music. Shambhala will murmur affirmations about world peace, saying be brave, be bold, be brilliant. At the end, everyone lies in corpse pose while Shambhala goes around and sprays eucalyptus oil over us. It's yoga as spa treatment.

Afterward I can steam and shower and slather myself with Kiehl's products, yet another form of exercise.

But no. There's a sub in for Shambhala.

It's Kelly, a tattooed African American former ballet dancer with a mellow voice of butter. Okay, he does seem very soothing.

"Intention," he says. "Start your day with a certain intention."

I like that it's 10:30 in the morning and we are "starting our day."

Saying "Om"—check.

Neck rolling because we slept wrong—check.

Downward-facing dog. My weak T-Rex arms wobble. It's a little strenuous. I hope we won't be here long.

For each pose, Kelly presents three versions. One is toe on ground. The second is toe slightly lifted. The third is a crazy pose that looks like a contortionist.

Some of these poses have weird names. I know child's pose and happy baby. But the frog, dolphin, scorpion, or most horribly of all, bird of paradise? Then there's the bridge into the wheel into the nuclear reactor or synchrotron.

Kelly offers one that goes like this: Lunge. Twist. Reach your arms around behind your back. I try to mimic what I saw the MILFs around me doing, but when I wrap my arms around my thigh there's this huge trunk of flesh and I can't think how to have my arms meet each other. I need a skinnier leg, or perhaps a half leg.

With a small yelp, I capsize.

I can't do easy yoga. I groan. I lie capsized on the floor.

# The Gynecologist

WORRIED WHETHER THERE'S something really wrong with me, something *osteoarthritical*, I break my three-year medical fast and go to the doctor.

I'm at that tender time of life where I avoid seeing the doctor because I can't face being weighed. For Pete's sake, it's hard enough in middle age to gather courage to face all those worrisome tests, scans, lab results. (But no, then they throw you onto the scale like a terrified piece of beef cattle and then slap a cuff on you and immediately take your blood pressure after you've just seen your actual weight in red digital letters— "Why is your blood pressure so high?" they wonder.)

Why can't doctors just glance at us, in our paper gowns, humiliating enough, and see whether our body types are active, medium, or relaxed fit? I acknowledge that there are pants I avoid, but I can still fit into my car to drive my kids. Why are doctors so curious to know our exact poundages? It's the twenty-first century! I have GPS in my phone. They should be able to wave a wand over us—and keep the exact data to themselves. Inside a large underground bunker somewhere. In Canada.

But then Marilyn gives me this great suggestion: "Just step on the scale backward—and ask them not to say your weight aloud."

So I do this and it works brilliantly! I bring out my inner middle-aged person monologue and hilariously regale all the nurses with my fears of being weighed, of dental work, and of flying, of mice. They're all in stitches about it.

"You're too much!" one says, while the other wipes tears of laughter and writes down some numbers on a clipboard. Come to think of it, they've got a few extra pounds as well. We should gather for a Groupon happy hour.

And then I laugh my way into my gown and onto the metal table—where my doctor is all about my weight.

"You want to know the number?" she says, leaning forward conspiratorially.

"No!"

She tells me anyway. I am the highest weight I've ever been, by a lot. The BMI has always seemed a relatively forgiving number, with a thirty-five-plus pound range of what's "normal" for me. . . .

But now my BMI has tipped up into "unhealthy." I am prediabetic.

I'm also way overdue for a colonoscopy.

When I freak out afterward to Julia, her words are reassuring: "I have to get a colonoscopy, too. We'll be colonoscopy partners. Because, good news, with all the flushing out, we'll lose all this weight!"

# Down the Tubes

OKAY, IT IS TIME TO GET A COLONOSCOPY. NOW!!!
Upon my statement of intention, I'm instantly sure something's wrong. I'm the sort of neurotic who secretly believes my actions control the universe. On airplanes, I hold the plane up by clutching the armrests. Remember the stock market dive of the 1990s? After seeing all my mutual funds plunge, I panicked and sold everything. Literally the very next day, the market recovered. Everything rose again, once I removed my small but plutonium-heavy anvil of funds. And you're welcome! America.

So, I take a deep shaky breath, pick up the phone, call the gastroenterologist, utter my name. I'm shocked and relieved when the receptionist doesn't immediately scream, "You're Sandra LOH? It's too late! Nooo!" Rather, she says it will take a few weeks to book the appointment, after I fill out some paperwork, which she'll send to me like she would any other normal person. Hurray!

But here's what happens. The colonoscopy paperwork arrives. It's like fifty pages long. This may well be the most complex part of a colonoscopy—stifling your panic while you fill out endless forms.

However, in the mess of my home, I somehow misplace my colonoscopy mini-Bible. In response to my fateful disorganization, my intestines (is that part of the colon?) feel like they're twisting and on fire.

After two weeks of hunting, I give up, call the office and order another set. I place it immediately into my glove compartment. I'm driving to a hospital in Palmdale to visit my dad, who's recuperating from a virus. Hours of boredom—a perfect opportunity for me to fill out my papers. I arrive at his bedside, pull out the forms, and realize my pen has run out of ink. "Nooooo!" I scream at the heavens, balling up my fists.

Unbelievably, I finally file the paperwork and am rewarded with a colon-cleaning "package" in the mail that includes Gatorade powder, chicken bouillon, and some other items too anatomically specific to mention. A date is set.

Thank God I have Julia! My Colonoscopy Partner! We're doing this together! Joining hands! Metaphorically—thank God we're doing this far from each other.

We cheerlead each other by phone: "You called the gastroenterologist! You made it through fifty pages of paperwork! You booked the appointment!"

For laughs, we send each other links to today's all-too-explicit medical websites. In one, a cartoon character shaped like a colon gives you a video tour of a real-life messy colon. Actual dialogue: "Think of it this way: a clean colon is like driving on a country road on a sunny day. A dirty colon is like driving in a snowstorm." Or actually, poop storm. This is a video I really wish I hadn't seen. Then I wonder whose colon starred in it. Do they know we're watching?

Those startling visuals are apparently what doctors feel they need to convince you to flush out your bowels properly. But there are some differences about how they interpret that.

"The week before, Dr. Wilson says, 'No fish oil, nuts, seeds,'"
I tell Julia.

"Really?" she says. "Dr. Abkarian says nothing about seeds, but
he says no trail mix and no red meat.' And the day before, while
drinking the flushing-out Gatorade stuff, it's a fast of clear liquids.
Tea, broth, water—"

"What about alcohol?" I ask.

"That's what many Americans are wondering," she says, "judg-
ing by the millions of Google searches. The most popular clear liquid
for colon cleansing is vodka. Many people combine it with Gatorade
as a mixer."

This may seem a rather dull conversation. . . .

But the morning of, as a friendly nurse tucks me in under my
blanket, she asks, "How was your prep? Everyone has a story!" She
wants to know how many fluid ounces I drank. At what hour my pee
turned what color. She is very, very fascinated.

Indeed, I am so flattered by the attention, I almost don't notice
when they start turning me to my side. "Hey wait a minute!" I
exclaim. And then I am out. At least for a bit. Either I hallucinated
this or I actually woke up in the middle, and found I was experiencing an annoying, pulling sensation à la Charlie's squeegee—"EE ee
EE ee EE!"

"Whoa!" I said. At which point it seemed like a small nun in a
big winged hat picked up a frying pan and clonked me over the head
with it.

The lesson being, perhaps? When you're getting anesthesia, don't
gloss over your weight, as I always do. Admit you weigh three hundred pounds.

# Going ~~Medieval~~ Atkins

THE *GREEN GODDESS COOKBOOK*. The Mediterranean Diet, the olive oil, the cheeses, the vegetables . . . which, quite frankly, we've started frying.

For months, I had been thinking, *Man—all these vegetables are filling— My stomach's bloated— All that fiber— But tomorrow nature's broom will come to the rescue!*

But it never does.

"Carbs," my gay friend Rick tells me. He's a vain sixtysomething who still has his boy body. "That's why I've switched from Bloody Marys to Bullshots—where instead of tomato juice you use beef boullion. Because those are the secret carbs—vegetables. You were telling me about your Brussels sprouts recipe? That's a carb per sprout! Eat twenty and you're done for the day!"

"Oh come on!" I say. "I refuse to fight with a grown man over how fattening Brussels sprouts are." I think it's the occasional triangle of reduced fat Laughing Cow cheese—an extra thirty calories— I add.

Determined to be good, I'm off to the farmer's market. But I'm

so hangry—aka, hungry and angry—and light-headed from the lack
of cheese, I forget I'm food shopping and find myself thinking more
like a geologist at a gem fair.

"Look at that rare and incredibly colorful item!" I say to myself,
bedazzled by the giant cauliflowers, in exotic colors like purple and
yellow and lime green. I drag a neon orange one home. Bigger than a
basketball, it won't go in the fridge. And so, with barely the strength
to wield a knife, I feebly attack the cauliflower, hacking away at it.
But when you stab a cauliflower it explodes into tiny florets that shoot
horizontally outward into every nook and cranny of your kitchen.

I need a Trader Joe's salad. But when I start really looking at
them, enriched with bulgur wheat and cranberries and quinoa? Oh
my God! It's like sixty-four carbs and forty-five grams of fat, due to
the miso soy peanut dressing! Not kidding. You can just consume a
tureen of macaroni and cheese and be better off.

At which moment, in the devil's sibilant whisper, a single dark
word floats: "Atkins."

I've never dared Atkins before. It is a measure of how frightened
I've become of fat that even the notion of consuming a single egg
yolk triggers heart palpitations. Dare I do it? Atkins is so politically
incorrect, it feels like you're making a pact with the devil. It feels like
you're clubbing baby seals with a giant Renaissance Faire turkey leg.
Which is in fact allowed, sans barbecue sauce.

Understand that in Phase One of Atkins, ominously called
"Induction," you cut out fruit! Why? Because it's packed with sugar.
After you've lost that first 150 pounds, you may try half an apple per
day. Maybe. Unless it causes the weight to fly back on. Vegetables are
also restricted. Broccoli and even lettuce are measured out a half cup
at a time. Carrots are a flat-out no.

Meanwhile, red meat? Woot, woot! It's a red meat festival! Red
meat you may have at every meal. Atkins does not mind if the cows

themselves were force-fed McDonald's while strapped in front of TVs watching bad reality shows featuring the Kardashians. Not only does Atkins not mind, Atkins invites you to top that red meat with bacon, eggs, and blue cheese because—that's right. No carbs! Woot, woot! You might add a tomato but it should be, as they say, and I quote, "a SMALL tomato."

Going from the low-fat quasi-vegetarian diet I had been on into the Devil's Lair of Atkins is surreal. As if in a dream, I find myself standing in my weekly farmer's market and realizing . . . I can't eat anything here! These colorful sample slices of peach, nectarine, Fuji apple? Corn and sweet potatoes? Vegan honey? Buckets of plutonium! What can I eat? Well, my friends, in slow motion, I crumple my canvas Trader Joe's bags, throw them into the Volvo, and drive myself to In-N-Out, where I order a protein style (no bun) Double-Double.

I have not had a cheeseburger in over ten years. It is a religious experience. And, horribly, I am so sorry to report? In a bit over a month, substituting a daily salad for lunch with an In-N-Out Double-Double, I dropped seven pounds. I'm not kidding. I do not know how this is possible. I have eaten so many In-N-Out burgers while driving, even when I make myself a snack in my kitchen, I find myself taking it out to the car so I can eat it over the steering wheel.

# In a Spin

Now I HAVE an amazing colon. I'm dropping weight. I have all this energy.

I'm entering a phase we might call Survivor's Guilt Olympics.

In the upswing of my bipolar mania, at my yuppie gym, I find myself drawn to the spinning room. I peer in through the glass. For as long as I can remember, it has been a regular, brightly lit workout room, with rows of bikes. Overnight, it has been transformed into a kind of disco, with black walls and flashing neon lights. What on earth goes on in there? Sometimes, at the end of a class, packed with sweaty, euphoric, middle-aged cyclists you'll see ghostly wall projections with people's names on them—"Ashley!"—next to how far they had biked— *To Tokyo!* I think. I didn't have my good glasses on. It seemed far. And international. And exciting.

I study the schedule. Spinning class at 6:30 a.m. is a bridge too far, even on Tokyo time. 8:30 a.m. seems more civilized, but you can't just walk in. You have to reserve a bike by downloading the gym's app— Check! And then clicking on the bike you want— But no, here it's the day before, and the class is already full! Yegads!

My competitive instincts are now strung out to the max. Mind you, I don't even know how to spin—and as I said, I hate biking. But the thought that I'm somehow being denied this magical experience is making me feel all jumpy and strung out and Lance Armstrong-y. Refreshing my browser and reading the fine print, I realize the booking window opens exactly twenty-six hours in advance! There's a digital clock ticking down! I grab a Powerade and ready myself to beat all the others! I will not be denied my spin.

So I am now setting my alarm the day before at 6:25 a.m. so I can book a bike at exactly 6:30. The alarm goes off, I zip downstairs to get my phone with the gym's app, zip back up to get back into bed. Then, with a scream, at 6:29 a.m., I realize I left my reading glasses downstairs. The print's too tiny to see. I sprint back down. I'm not even in the saddle and my heart rate is up to 150! But—

Ding! I'm in!

At 6:31 there are two bikes left, and one is mine, mine, mine!

I arrive the next morning, amped up, even though I have no idea how to spin. Sonya, our Amazon-like spinning instructress, approaches me. She asks whether I am wearing cycling shoes. I do not know what those are. No matter. She fetches metal toe-holders that look like tiny bear traps. I'm getting in deep.

All the arriving cyclists are very excited. No one is under the age of forty-five. No matter: all wear cut-off shirts and bike pants and backward caps. They're a team. And here we go, cycling, to the B-52's "Love Shack." Sonya exhorts us to greet one another and exchange high-fives.

"Woo hoo!" everyone yells. I've discovered a cult! I love it!

"Go to 70 percent of your max!" Sonya cries out. "Play with your edge!" I ignore that and just continue on the easiest gear possible.

Point being: I'm spinning!

I sing along to the next tune, Duran Duran, no apologies: "Her name is Rio and she dances on the sand!"

# Getting Sirius

I REMEMBER ONE TIME being very annoyed with my engineer
friend Ned. His house's solar panels made electric energy, which in
turn powered his Tesla: "So I'm driving on sun!" I was forced to watch
a video screen of Ned's car's extremely self-congratulatory energy
system. Arrows fussily flowed around the engine as if to say, "Hey,
look what I'm doing now!" Ned excitedly showed me how when we
were going downhill: "I am literally making electricity. Right now."
Never mind that every twenty-nine miles you have to "plug the car
in" so it could quietly commune with its Martian brethren.

But Costco is amazing.

My Volvo has been dying and . . .

Just for this month, there's a crazy deal where I can lease a hybrid
electric Chevy Volt for under $200 a month, and get $700 in Costco
cash *and* a several thousand dollar rebate from the state of California.

The government Jerry Brown made is essentially paying me to
drive clean. With my clean colon. I'm printing money—or at least
Costco cash!

But driving my new Volt, I get confused very quickly.

"It doesn't go in reverse!" I scream at Charlie, trying to back out of the driveway. I am anxiously tapping the gas and revving it and pumping the brake and I still can't hear the engine. "What's wrong with this car?"

"I think you need to give it power!" he yells.

"Aha!"

Now that I know how to drive it, I immediately become smug myself. I feel so virtuous when I'm on electricity, like such a failure when we go to gas.

But my pains are assuaged by Sirius XM radio, the music service for old people. They have stations like:

"The Bridge"
"The Coffeehouse"
"Shoes Off Radio." Shoes off!
"Margaritaville," which is all Jimmy Buffett (and why not?)
Or just, you know, "the Eagles."

This is SO my demographic—they are channeling my inner thoughts! But mostly I do the mixes, like:

"Real Jazz"
When that's *too* real, I switch to adult contemporary . . .
"Watercolors"
Too distractingly splashy? Now comes. . .
"Spa"
Too edgy?
How about "Nail Spa"? *Yes!*

With my Jamaican Rum Yankee Candle car air freshener, I'll never leave the Hotel California!

# Me and My Massage Chair

A S IF IN A continual waking dream, here I am again. Costco.
    I have been coming to Costco for twenty-five years. My adult life has been defined by the stages of Costco. So many memories are from here. The first time I took my dad's Chinese wife Helen here, how she ran down the halls in her white tennies, afraid the bargains would be snatched away. The time Hannah and Sally's cousin Wayne, small enough at two to be seated in the cart, suddenly let loose an explosion of pee over the Capri tomatoes with a sound like shattering glass. The time a teen Hannah and I caught our first Pokémon GO Ninetales in the returns line.

I step into the entry "gallery" in the Glendale Costco, eternally curious. Look at these wonderfully strange products!

The green Canadian-made duffle bags that won't quite fit into airline overhead compartments (I've made that mistake). Lady's Power Stretch Capris (four words that should not be in the same sentence). VSOP cognac. Boogie boards. I remember one time there were actually coffins.

But then I see IT. My heart stops.

Before I describe IT, let's take a step back.

I admit I am a massage glutton. I'm the sort of person who wonders why, like Madonna, I may not get a massage every day. When I do treat myself to this "luxury," a slightly skanky Groupon 30-percent-off angle is typically involved. It's akin to being handed a fluffy spa robe and towel, but only one slightly moldy spa sandal.

Most recently, I've opted for mall "chair massages."

Oh yes. You know the type of place. It's not an actual spa with private rooms. It's like those quickie-massage places you see in airports. Here, a handful of defeated-looking pedestrians in their street clothes slump over chairs, towels over their backs, all dignity surrendered. Depressed-looking attendants in polo shirts rub their shoulders while gazing woodenly into the middle distance. It's a veritable land of Unhappy Endings.

"The Massage Store" . . . Like "Nighthawks," it should be the subject of an Edward Hopper painting, everyone's skin in greenish tones.

Anyway, for years, like you, I'd pass these massage-on-the-go places and I would feel sorry for the sad-sack rubes who would risk infection and disease for the touch of a sullen stranger.

But then, you know what? Overnight I became one of those people! I went to the mall telling myself I was only picking up Charlie's annual (because it is thirty-four dollars) bottle of Kiehl's shampoo. But then, feigning self-surprise, I found myself suddenly zigzagging left into "Healing Hands."

How did it go? To be honest, fifteen minutes later, I felt as besmirched—and yet as secretly elated—as if I had just used Tinder. The beauty is that the transaction is so simple, and clear. There are no appointments. You just walk in and, within sixty seconds, no questions asked, Asian—yes, they are—masseurs drape you over a chair with a—hopefully—clean towel on it and start massaging your shoulders.

It's so much better than a relationship—which I always experience as way too much talk and way too little massage.

Kaitlin, of course, destroyed my bubble: "Do you know how much those people make? Do the math! They're charging twelve dollars to rub your body. Since most of the overhead goes to the store and management, someone is getting four dollars to palpate your flabby arms. Don't you feel violated? You're certainly violating them. It's like those Korean foot massage places, human sweatshops with little gray towels so worn out you can't even see the Chi symbol on them."

"Well, I did feel guilty," I protest, "of course I did. But I tip them like 40 percent!"

"Which is like five dollars!"

"But it's still 40 percent," I repeat, my cheeks flushing in confusion. But never mind all that.

Because, here now, at Costco, the granter of dreams, is . . . The Massage Chair.

The chocolate-colored leatherette behemoth-like Osaki 2000. $2,999.

My very own Eurobear. My Sugar Daddy. Waiting for me to get on his lap.

It sits before a case of engagement rings. As though to say, after the engagement, after many years, you will need the massage chair. Although to be honest, at Costco, what with the salad spinners next to beach towels, no narrative can really be read.

True, Sally and I once saw a dead man at Costco. There was a sheet over a body with wee man's dress shoes sticking out by the printer ink. The EMTs packing him up were unhurried. Although I, too, feel I sometimes can't go on after comparing laser printer inks.

The only problem is that there's a twenty-year-old Latino guy in cargo shorts already auditioning the chair. His expression is masked behind dark, wrap-around sunglasses, gently vibrating.

When I circle back ten minutes later, now there is an Armenian grandmother, with purplish hair downy as a chicken's, hanging on for dear life. Her daughter, in blue Lycra leggings, holding a baby, lecturing, is making her do it. It looks like grandma needs a seat belt. Her hands gripping the Osaki are like claws. She is not happy.

I circle away again to get a giant tub of Fancy Mixed Nuts. And when I return?

The massage chair is free.

There is no Purel in sight, and no matter. Massage chairs. Not for the shy. I settle down in the still-warm vessel, ass cheeks lightly clenched.

I lift the magic remote. Click on "Relax."

Like a miniature Skylab, or robotic clam shell, the massage chair groans and tilts my feet up, head backward. This is serious.

It encloses me in its soft leatherette labial folds.

Whining rollers begin on my back and shoulders. This is very good. Shiatsu. Deep tissue.

Now pincers close on my arms, irrevocably. "You're going nowhere," the chair seems to say. The pressure is not entirely unpleasant. I give in to it.

With a moan, this rolling bar descends from my neck and shoulders, down my spine, to my butt.

Oh my God.

It's not like I see God, but a portal opens.

The emotion is intense. I want to get on bended knee and propose marriage to the Osaki. In the original German. And present it with a formal bouquet, like *Der Rosenkavalier*.

My hip feels amazing. I exhale with that long sensual sigh heard only by the middle-aged people assuming child's pose in yoga.

But $2,999. Too much!

In line, a Costco guy named Alberto catches up with me. "Just for today," he says, "I can mark the Osaki down $1,000 to $1,999!"

And here's the thing—I can use $700 in Costco cash Jerry Brown gave me for my electric car! I'm printing money!

Anyway: you can't take it with you.

The assembly almost kills us, in particular, Charlie, who has to crawl under it to attach the footrest, whose collapse would literally crush his skull.

But from then on, I know pleasure.

Middle age: it's not so bad.

Each night I sit in the massage chair with a glass of wine.

In Sirius radio from the big computer come the gentle tones of the Spa Channel. While my new Roomba (also on sale) vacuums.

Instead of guilt-making Third World help, I have happy robots.

#winning.

I am at peace.

# Villager Number 31

## "Storm of Joy"

AND SO IT GOES, another fall.

Hannah took the SAT, texted me the results. She is happy with her "Second-tier-UC-possibly-a-hair-below-average" score. When I make her take it a second time three months later, she will score ten points *lower*, and will refuse to take it again. And scene.

Meanwhile, Sam is at community college. Thriving. Tiger Aunt reports: "For the first time in years, Sam is sleeping eight hours a night and is awake for all of his classes. He has put his schedule on an Excel spreadsheet and is getting straight As. He's pulling it together."

He even has time to help others.

Hannah has some AP bio homework so confounding she's not objecting to help. I post the problem on our family e-mail thread of ten people. This includes my computer programmer brother, my sister, her scientist husband, UC Davis physics professor "Uncle" Greg . . .

Even the adults are confused by the problem, but Sam jumps right in, quite coherent:

*In the first picture she has the wrong sign for the .3M. The core increased in mass (positive), not decreased (negative). The point is that everything wants to find equilibrium (a balance point). Example: If I was driving through Alaska during the winter and I opened my window, the temperature inside my car would drop until it was roughly the outdoor temperature. If I were to open the window while driving through Death Valley in summer, the temperature inside the car would increase. If I open the window while driving through PG, I just get the wind whipping through my hair.*

*Why not start there and if there's still confusion I can try explaining more?*

*Sincerely,*

*Rarely too busy to help a cousy*


(Where was he when Sally and I were doing middle school biology?)


So: A FINAL TALE about Hannah.

As enlightened modern parents, we would no sooner spank our children than be naysayers to them. To crush their dreams. And yet, with each child born in America, there comes the moment when they thrillingly declare, with shining eyes: "I am going to be the youngest kid ever to win twelve Olympic gold medals!"

The emotion is so pure. The clouds part, the sun shines. Your son or daughter or beloved other beholds their certain-to-be glorious future.

In the face of such optimism, who are we to smash their dreams?

But in fact, the reasonable response is "Yes, and although you're fairly young—nine? Small complication is that you've never been in a swimming pool. Not that I don't, er . . . believe in you." Because it's your job to keep them from actually drowning.

So, back at age ten, Hannah caught the acting bug.

In elementary school, she had been the shyest in her class. She could barely muster the courage to sing Christmas carols, Santa hat over her eyes. In dance class, if she made one wrong step, she'd collapse in the corner like a noodle, weeping.

But for some unexplained reason, Hannah thought a "performing arts academy" for middle school sounded like fun.

Small problem? An audition. For sixth grade.

When I look at the audition "guidelines" my bowels turn to ice.

In just two weeks, because we got started so late, my noodle-like daughter is expected to perform, without laughing:

A one-minute dramatic monologue
A one-minute excerpt from a Broadway musical
A dance combination

"Attach photo and résumé?" I cry out. "My God! What happened to childhood? She just wants to run around an auditorium holding a tree branch!"

Never mind getting into the school, which is beyond our control. My main worry is that the audition itself will be a traumatic childhood experience.

So as usual: I construct the facade of a pleasant, measured, confident person.

I begin by giving my Gen Z daughter a crash course in The Broadway Musical. "Hannah, do you remember that Will Ferrell movie where he's jumping through lava and singing 'God, I hope I get it'? Or when Sponge Bob sings, 'Where have all the staplers gone?'

Or when the Simpsons—? Anyway!" I conclude brightly. "Those are all parodies of Broadway musicals."

There is one she is familiar with: *Cats.*

The song: "Memories." Fine!

In the—yes—now ten days we have to prepare for the audition, I instigate a kind of Broadway homeschool program. Instead of *Fame* HIGH school, think *Fame* HOME school.

In the morning, we do stretches and short dance routines I make up on the fly—step step STEP turn! Step step CLAP turn!

I coach her on announcing herself: " 'Today I will be performing a monologue from *Love, Loss and What I Wore* by Nora Ephron.' No," I correct myself, "even better, say 'by the great'—and then take a beat and give a big smile—'Nora Ephron.' "

She will be auditioning for a drama teacher named Rivka Mandelbaum—you think Jewish, yes?

"Memories" from *Cats* is still a problem, because Hannah and I cannot agree on what the melody actually is, but no matter.

DIANA ROSS FAMOUSLY had a tunnel built from the wings to the stage so she didn't have to look at the little people. Unfortunately, in Hannah's case the "little people" include her sister. There's no room for a tent in our then-Volvo back seat. As Hannah chimes "Mem'ries!" for the hundredth time, Sally screams, "Go to middle school already and get out of my life!"

IT'S THE DAY OF the audition. My shoes are pinching me. I've come dressed as a Stage Mom, in uncharacteristic blouse, skirt, and heels. I've got on lipstick and a red hair band. The school should know this future star's mother is ready to bake cookies, fund-raise, usher, write personal checks, scrub tiny junior high school toilets!

But now we arrive and I see a terrifying vision. Fifty other stage moms and their daughters, all feverishly running their lines. (Is that the sound of "Mem'ries"?)

*Oh no!* I think. *To get into acting school, my daughter forgot to be a . . . boy!* Hannah doesn't feel horrible afterward. She says her song and monologue went okay, and she flubbed the dance, but so did some other people.

To my absolute amazement, she gets in! But now, the horrible experience begins.

Because this turns out to be the Cruel Performing Arts Middle School (CPAMS). For the next three years, Hannah does not say one line on stage ever. CPAMS turns out to be this Studio City wormhole where parents in the entertainment industry send their kids. These pint-sized professionals have had head shots since second grade and it's a total nightmare.

The stars are the same three to five kids over and over again. We're talking the kids who have won the genetic lottery by evading any of the acne, weight gain, metal braces, or general loss of center of gravity that typically comes with adolescence.

Chaotic dance recitals with canned music would typically star the dance teacher's daughter Sierra. Sierra had maintained the ninety-pound gamine-like frame of her girlhood and could do showy gymnastics in a style we might call "sexy cat."

At the annual "all-school" dance show, Hannah and literally seventy-five other girls would run out on stage, not even in straight lines. They would do a bit of a Charleston and lift one another and that was their whole number.

This is the exact opposite of how Tiger Mom Amy Chua raised her daughters. Tiger Mom thought playing "Villager Number 7" in the school play was a waste of time. At CPAMS, we would have been *thrilled* if Hannah got to play "Villager Number 7"!

But since Hannah loved theater so much, she still wanted to be part of the production. So she worked on crew, delighting in her wireless headset. Even though it meant you had to stay an hour after the actors left and pick up their costumes like Cinderella.

As Hannah said, "CPAMS destroyed my dream."

FOR NINTH GRADE, Hannah's neighborhood school becomes Big Urban High School (BUHS). It does not have the same stellar reputation as CPAMS, where *everyone* wants to go. But I'm thinking, *Hey, wait a minute. Let's send her to the "mediocre" performing arts academy and maybe she'll get to speak a line ever.*

But while a bit ghetto-looking from the outside, BUHS is not at all mediocre. Head of the theater department is Mr. Wells, a Vietnam war vet turned drama teacher. He rules his kids with military precision. This goes beyond showing up and being on time, about which he is manic. (To this day, I've never seen any producer start a 3:00 p.m. performance at 2:55.) It's about rehearsing and rehearsing and rehearsing. That's until 6 p.m. every weekday, then six hours every Saturday.

When is there time to do the homework you need to, for . . . UCLA? (And would you like fries with that?)

So Hannah goes and auditions for the play, Shakespeare's *As You Like It.*

I stand on the sidewalk, look up into the sky and say, "Please, God. Give her any speaking part."

And astonishingly, she gets the very last part with a name. Audrey. Six lines. Eventually cut to four. But she . . . gets a part!

Now come auditions for the musical, her bête noire. Hannah

rehearses for it with her two girlfriends. They practice together in the living room. They're adorable.

Her two friends get cast. Hannah doesn't.

"Oh honey," I say, "at least you'll have a lot more time for your schoolwork."

"Oh no, mom," she says. "I'm going to go to the rehearsals anyway. To learn the show just in case anyone drops out."

But indeed, there's a guy playing A Drunk who has three lines. Due to the long rehearsal hours for so few lines, he sensibly drops out. Hannah suggests to Mr. Wells that she could play the Drunk as a female, because she's there every day anyway.

He says he'll think about it.


A COUPLE OF DAYS LATER, he says no.

Her spirits are flagging, but she keeps turning up.

And then suddenly another girl drops out and Mr. Wells puts Hannah in! And so it goes. She gets a good part, a bad part, a lead, an extra. . . .

And now comes the big musical—*Beauty and the Beast*.

She knows shooting for Belle is a reach, but is hoping that, because of her comic timing, she might have a shot at Lumiere.

The text:

**LOL, Mom. I got cast as "Chorus Girl Number Five."**

I type back:

**Congratulations! Five is the best one, honey. You wouldn't want to be Chorus Girl Number Two, or Four.**

Months of endless rehearsals follow. Time that could have been spent *studying for the SATs. Grinding down on those maps for AP world history.*

I maintain hope that a youthful passion for theater transitions into lucrative management consulting or an amazing corporate sales career. ("It's global synergy, innovative products, engaged customers!")

But just as likely not.

And yet.

And yet.

On the upside, I'm developing new skills. I've discovered how to use my iPad as "the Hannah Cam." To wit: Among thirty chorus kids running around on stage, I'm always able to frame my kid in the exact center of the shot, as though she were the actual star. It takes some effort. In the big dance number "Be Our Guest!" I keep muttering, "Okay, Belle, enough singing, step aside!" or, "Yes, teacup girl, we get it—you can jump up and do the splits! You're blocking my quietly seated daughter" or, "Oh no. Here it comes to obscure everyone—a frickin' giant twirling cake!"

But then for some reason, the video doesn't save. I end up going to the show four times, to try to get it right.

There are Tiger Moms, Panda Moms, Sloth Moms. (What's below UC Merced?) I'm the mom who drove her daughter to all the rehearsals for her flyspeck part, and who can't even manage to get decent amateur video.

And yet.

And yet.

High school theater is its own kind of magic.

The following year, the musical is Cole Porter's *Anything Goes.* Hannah is in the chorus, without any numerical distinction at all. But perhaps it's the most magical performance.

Picture yourself driving up gritty Van Nuys Boulevard past taco trucks and tattoo parlors. At the end of the street, a lit auditorium beckons. A live orchestra is warming up. How did they manage to gather thirty musicians at the Big Urban High School? Because that's its big urban spirit: you can enter in ninth grade with no musical training, and they'll start teaching you where you are.

Roll of timpani, lights up . . .

There are fifty kids on stage, in curled hair and 1930s costumes, on a massive cruise ship!

It's a cinematic thrill! The audience bursts into applause.

The songs are classic: "Anything Goes," "It's De-Lovely," "Let's Misbehave."

My daughter's exact role doesn't matter (I have, in any case, given up on videotaping). The point is, fifty kids of all colors, shapes, and sizes get to sing and dance. There's some deftly choreographed Busby Berkeley stuff (crowds can be precise when a Vietnam veteran is drilling them). The tapping has this insane verve. Even the smallest roles are full of brio. A small blonde boy in a yachting cap two sizes too big runs around the edges of a crowd scene as if to say, "I am the purser! I am the purser! This ringing of this ship's bell is very important!"

Every night, the chorus members and crew backstage act out the scenes taking place on stage, switching out who plays the stars.

Our Second World children are perhaps neither elites nor victims. What are they?

A storm of joy.

# Thanksgiving

I T'S DEEP, deep autumn.

Every twilight is like one of those Magritte paintings, with the dark houses in front and silhouette trees and lit-up sky behind them, fading.

It's the most beautiful time of the year. Also, inexplicably, the saddest.

Typically, every year I take the girls to see grandpa in the morning, and then bring them back to their dad's for them to have Thanksgiving in the evening.

This year, Thomas has taken my dad to see some of Thomas's growing extended family in San Diego. There's not much actual Thanksgiving feasting these days, in any case, with my dad's GI tube.

So we just went out for breakfast this morning at Du-par's (open every day of the year) and now I've dropped them off.

As usual, when I drop them off, the door opens and closes, as though by an unseen hand. Perhaps an errant "Happy Thanksgiving!" is tossed out, or piece of misdelivered mail.

Usually I would speed back to Pasadena, but today, I can't bear to, just yet. The emotion of November hangs on me.

I sit in my parked car and look back at my old house.

Ben keeps it in great shape. There are always pleasing updates to admire. The driveway is newly asphalted, bushes are trimmed, the garden gate, at the left, has just been repainted.

I remember all the Thanksgivings of the past, here.

I remember when my father, sister, and brother, all the Lohs, descended on what is now my ex-husband's house. We put two tables together lengthwise in our small but warm living room. That year, Ben did a Julia Child recipe. It took days of preparation, pureeing chicken livers with sweet butter and dolloping it all sensually on toast points. There were four pies (pumpkin, apple, blueberry, cherry) and a cheesecake.

The meal was so rich, my father fainted at the table. We had to call 911.

That said, everyone was pretty jolly about it. My sister snapped photos as buff EMTs strapped my dad onto a gurney. My brother continued to eat, taking over my father's portions. My father had sustained so many emergency room visits over the years, it was its own holiday ritual.

Now Christmas is coming. I'm both relieved but also a touch sad to see that Sally, the youngest child of the five grandchildren, she of the much-hated pants, infelicitously positioned stuffed animals, and forever-lost toothpaste caps, has set the bar quite low for Santa this year. Wasn't it just three years ago that she demanded we rig a video camera so she could get photographic evidence of Santa? (Which we did: the live—if dark and blurry—footage shows a fat man in a red suit scrambling out of the fireplace and letting forth a dramatic startled "What the—?" And if Santa sounds a little like Charlie—that's the magic.)

No, this year, curiously: "I just want a booklet of cookie recipes with Post-its showing Santa's favorites," she has said, acknowledging, without acknowledging, her transition into teenhood.

I look at our old living room picture window, its big square panes framed in green, eggshell curtains. I remember Ben and me sitting there, in front of that picture window, now almost ten years ago, telling our little girls we were getting a divorce.

I remember their feet, so little, hanging off the couch.

Did it have to be that way? How many hours have I missed with them? Half their lives.

For years, I have told myself that being a divorced mom has been an unexpected blessing.

When I lived here, Ben often traveled almost half the year, so I was essentially a solo parent. Not thinking things through, I wrote full-time at home with no child care (that would be outsourcing motherhood) to the 24/7 crunch of Trader Joe's Pirate Booty and blare of *Dora the Explorer* (they're learning Spanish!). Instead of quality time, it was poor quality time. (Or do we call that quantity time?)

I would type on my laptop and throw—what else is in this pantry?—stale Halloween candy at my daughters and beg them to continue watching television.

Astonishingly, what parenting experts don't tell you is that eventually Second World children find television boring. Into the fifth hour, they would snap it off of their own accord. So I would devise the sorts of meaningless time-wasting games you might for pets. "Here's a roll of Bounty paper towels. Tear them up into tiny pieces." "Let's play a game called Let's Go into Mommy's Purse and Wash All Her Change." "Let's put on a princess dress and heels and run on mommy's treadmill." Someone has to.

But no, my girls always wanted all of us to do projects together, to bake cookies and squeeze lemonade. But I could barely keep the cooking and laundry and driving together. I could barely keep us in milk and underwear. The thought of the exploding flour and sticky lemons and seventeen-piece juicer? It was too much to contemplate.

In short, upon splitting up our household, when I had my girls just 50 percent of the time, I had gazelle intensity. I was able to Bring on the Mom they never had. I helped them with homework, drew baths, rubbed backs. We've done things once thought unimaginable—like going bowling and miniature golfing and to country fairs. We baked cookies and carved jack-o'-lanterns—one year, as an experiment, we carved one out of a pineapple, just to see what would happen. The first time we sparked up my new Target juicer and let it rip, it was like finding Narnia.

I WONDER WHETHER that's just a story I tell myself, though.

Because in the depths of November, I see there's no rerolling the film. Quality time or not, it's all just time.

# The Gardening Fairy

S UDDENLY, IN THE MIDST of what seems a year of eternal orangey psychic dusk, global warming, and unpredictable wildfires, the heavens open and it rains. A lot.

I would like to be able to say at this point, to passersby of our front yard: "Shield your eyes—I don't want you to be blinded by my wildflowers." But no. Perhaps my wildflowers, like my basil, have their own internal clock. To incubate, they need a few more months/seasons/years/millennia.

As the weeks go by, though, we do start marveling over the grass, which is now almost waist high. I use the word "grass," but in fact this greenery looks subtropical. There are teardrop-shaped leaves and thick leathery stems and twisting vines and clover.

"Is that what it's called, you think?" I ask Sally. "Clover?"

"Whatever it is, I think it's pretty."

"Overall, we are not displeased with our front yard, are we?"

"It's nice and green!"

"Which reflects well on us."

"As if the rain were a personal talent of ours."

But it is looking a tad, well, wild and unkempt, so Sally and I decide we are going to attack it, together. I will pay her twelve dollars an hour, like a real job. We have absolutely no idea what we are doing, but we're not going to seize up in panic about that. We're going to relax—ice to water, water to air—and be very Zen.

I suggest we need a holistic gardening "gestalt," à la . . .

"Everything green is fine. Our gardening knowledge is adequate. We don't need to know more. An ankle-high carpet of green is satisfactory."

"Wherever there are flowers," Sally agrees, "we leave them."

"Exactly. It's like an English garden concept."

Our garage boasts a rusty push mower, Weedwacker, and some buckets with moldy sponges in them, presumably for car washing, which also hasn't been done for a while.

*Where did we get those mannequins?* I wonder in passing as I pull out our tools. The Weedwacker lacks the bright blue plastic string that does the whacking. No matter. I pull my laptop onto the deck and wikiHow: "How to restring your weed eater." Two grainy YouTube videos later I give up. Might as well try to knit a pussy hat.

I take the Weedwacker to True Value. Happily, near the paint aisle, there's an orange-vested staffer with a beard and round belly, like a friendly local beaver. Restringing Weedwackers is his particular art. Hello, Tenth Husband.

"First you have to find the eyehole," is I think what he says, "and the number two grommet, and then flip it over to dig in here for the key nut—"

"Really?" I say, eyes wide. "Wow." Fueled by my intense interest, he now in fact flips it over to dig in for the key nut. "No way," I say, "cool." My sincere awe blossoms into surprised gratitude as, while continuing to narrate what I *should* do, he methodically restrings the entire Weedwacker himself, free of charge. I am thrilled.

When I return, I find Sally, in an improvised "farming" costume—overalls, red bandana, and flowered sombrero, weeding, with pure focused attention. But she is doing so one weed at a time, excavating them by the roots, almost as if she has named each one ("Jeannette!" "She was my best friend!"). At this rate, half our planet's species will be extinct before our yard is done. Since we lack gardening gloves (Charlie used them for a Hindu fire pit) to protect her hands, Sally is literally using an orange cloth dinner napkin from Cost Plus. It's like she's "massaging" the weeds out, as one might pull warm baguettes out of a country oven.

"You have to cut that—snip it," I say, fumbling for the vocabulary. But we don't have any of those—what are they? Choppers? All I can find in the house to cut things are kitchen shears, a nail file, and a pizza wheel.

Oh boy, this is getting more and more pathetic. Instead of a rake, we have a back-scratcher. What will we attack our plants with next? A Swiffer? Egg beaters? Febreze? Chopsticks? Shoehorns?

Our helplessness is too much. From across the street, from the fussy "Green Arrow Award" house itself, our Herculean Latino neighbor Lorenzo, in hefty-weight jeans and sparkling white T-shirt, rumbles toward us. He is pushing a gigantic red Toro power mower. Hello, Eleventh Husband!

"Hey, neighbor!" he calls out, all business. "I'll be done in five minutes."

He rips the cord. There's a roar.

Sally and I are startled. And ashamed. Also grateful. But—we shoot each other a look—should we tell him about our gestalt English garden plan, to leave the charming mini flower meadows as they lay, maybe go around them? No! As his machine roars right over them! He is crushing our dream!

But, disturbingly, huge insects are flying out. First butterflies and ladybugs, but then weird bees and weird not-quite-bees. We hear the shuh-duh-duh-duh-duh of wings. I'm actually a little spooked.

"Mosquitoes," he rumbles. "Tonight there will be mosquitoes. That's why you have to keep it cut."

Oh. Darker moment. It's clear we've been not just a neighborhood embarrassment but a danger!

Done with the mowing, now our hero rolls over an actual weed edger. It's like having wikiHow, live, in front of you.

I bring him a tall glass of water. He quaffs it, hurls away the ice, magnificently, continues with his labors.

And indeed, within fifteen minutes, incredibly, a front lawn appears. It is a beautiful, rectangular, neat, straight male thing.

"To thank him," I tell Sally, "we should bake some cookies."

She agrees: "Knowing us, he won't expect them to be good."

And we give thanks, today, for our Gentle Gardening Giant.

# Mr. Loh's Not Afraid to Be Naked

"**Y**OUR PHONE HAS been going off."

Charlie hands me my coffee, tosses the *New York Times* on the bed. I look at the digital clock on my bedstand. It's 6:37 a.m.

Both girls are with me, under my roof. I can hear the chatter of media, bursts of song, showering.

There's no late-breaking scandal I'm involved with. No international incident is hitting the wires.

There's no possible job that would have any "coasts" urgently calling me. This is not *Mission Impossible*. I'm not a spy. Not a firefighter. Not . . .

"Did you see who?"

Charlie takes the phone out of his bathrobe pocket. "Your sister, and Thomas."

"Oh."

And in that moment, I know. My ninety-seven-year-old father has died.

If my dad had just been rushed to the hospital, there might be one frantic call from Thomas en route. But the calls would not keep coming, in sonar-pinging succession.

With the extremely old, there's a pattern. Typically, there's the emergency home event—a fall, sudden shortness of breath, failure to stir. From the urgent care unit, bedside, there's the rapid medical litany: "His pulse is low, he's drawing in just 10 percent of his own oxygen, his renal system is failing. . . ."

For normal adults this would seem fatal. But by ninety-seven, so many things have been falling off my dad for so many years. He's like Charlie's VW Beetle, whose driver's-seat armrest is currently secured with duct tape, front bumper held on with zip ties.

Which is to say, as has happened so often, immediately, a battery of devices are strapped onto my dad, pumping him with oxygen, chemicals, fluids. There's a twenty-four-hour wait-and-see "stabilization" period where there are no updates—we have time to soberly shower, snack, put on our "ER face"—and then, with a deep breath, push open those swinging doors. . . .

And literally every time, my dad would mysteriously reemerge. Or at least, various levels on the machines would drift back into green.

Never quite managing to graduate, my father has failed out of hospice three times. As a life form, my father is like a kind of alga.

In short, when considering the notion of his death, I feel just slight relief. Amazement.

*I literally didn't know he had it in him*, I think.

I take my time and finish the Monday *New York Times* crossword. Sadly, today it only takes eight minutes. Both KenKens take all of two minutes. That's the end of my escape pod. I can't hold off the day any longer.

I sigh and listen to my three messages, one from my sister, one from Thomas, then another from my sister. My father has indeed died, that morning, just after six. Thomas and Kaitlin sound a little breathy, lightly sad. No one is hysterical.

I feel nothing. It's like if someone said, "Oh, I paid your parking ticket."

"In fact," I say to Charlie, "if there's anyone who was to be found dead on this sunny Monday morning, my father is first in line."

I call my sister, who says I don't have to do anything. The necessary phone calls have been made, the coroner will come, he will issue a death certificate. That's the key document, which will trigger the estate stipulations, life insurance, benefits. Thomas has a lot to do, so I might just be in his way.

While Charlie is driving the girls to school, upon thinking about it, I decide I will make the seventy-five-minute drive, mostly for moral support of Thomas. He will definitely be the most traumatized. For the last eight years, he has been housing and caretaking my father. They are close. Also, now Thomas is going to lose anywhere between $7,000 and $12,000 a month in income. (It varied a bit—after a while, I just put my hands over my eyes.)

I drive to Palmdale on a beautiful morning, enjoying the mountain views of the Angeles Crest Highway.

The Chevy Volt screen jumps to life. Incoming phone call. ANDIE. Her slightly underwater-sounding voice beams into the cabin.

"Okay," she says. "I think I finally finally have a drought-resistant gardener for you."

"Great. Just text me the number. My dad just died."

"Oh no! Honey! I'm so sorry! Are you okay?"

"I feel weirdly calm," I say, winging through slopes of burned forest that, due to the recent rains, are just beginning to green. "I'm just admiring nature's plan. You just can't be upset, when someone with Parkinson's, who basically sleeps all the time, dies. In fact, considering how screwed up the world is, with war and school shootings and all the madness? How elegant for this gentleman to check out, leaving a full suite of kids and grandkids intact, shutting off the giant money leakage of his care, making a bit more room on the planet, first thing on a Monday morning, gettin' it done."

"I know. But it's your father. You only have one. You must be feeling sad."

"Well, I'm not. It's one of the best things he has ever done. The timing is great. I've just filed an article. Both my Monday and Tuesday are free. Thank you, dad!"

I PULL UP TO Thomas's brown and beige ranch-style house in Palmdale.

A police car is parked at the curb. No sirens. There's a sleepy, Mayberry-like feeling in this scene. The cop might as well be having a sandwich or a nap.

This death is overstaffed.

The front door opens and Thomas runs out. He looks stricken, like he has been wildly weeping. I see his face and am glad I came. His wife, Nina, runs out behind him, also looking stricken. We hug each other.

I enter Thomas's house. It's pleasantly cool, with its fancy black leatherette furniture, giant-screen TV, massive fish tank, huge faux-Grecian vases of artificial flowers. There are usually a few addled seniors in wheelchairs around, but today they have been moved to his other house.

A foam mattress is on the floor. A cream-colored blanket is covering a small, prone form, with feet in clean fluffy white socks sticking out at the bottom. A candle flickers nearby on a TV table.

Even the socks look snowy. That's Thomas's art. He has always kept my dad so fluffed and buffed, possibly only in the way you can when your charges are not really sentient.

"Do you want to see him?" Thomas whispers. I don't particularly. To be polite, though, I make a grateful face and say yes. Thomas lifts the blanket.

There is my dad. He looks much as he does when sleeping, but he's definitely a lighter shade of yellow. He has that distinctive pinched, hollowed-out look around the mouth that my mother had in death two decades earlier. My mom's death was more tragic, occurring in a nightmarish convalescent home when she was just sixty-nine, and all of us children still so young (in our thirties!). That said, coming a brutal ten years after her early Alzheimer's diagnosis at fifty-nine, the sad relief of her death was just as welcome.

I put my hand on his forehead. It's impossibly smooth, and still pretty warm. With a start, I realize, catching him just a few hours after death, I can still feel some of his warmth, the last life that is leaving him.

Not quite knowing what else to do, I decide to lie down next to my dad and take a selfie. With surprise but support, Thomas literally applauds the idea. "Sure, sure," he says, taking my phone. I crouch down and arrange myself next to my frail, inert father. He is smaller than me at this point. It is like lying next to a doll. Thomas snaps a photo of me with my dad, then we change places and I snap some photos of him and Thomas.

In the photos, my dad is yellow, like a melon. His fingers are curled talons, like a type of Asian fruit literally called "Buddha's Hand." All is an empty shell. The soul has left his body.

WHILE WAITING FOR the funeral home director to come, I think back again to when my mother died twenty-two years ago.

The doctor informed us of her "gradual electrical systems failure." We all arrived, my father and his (second Chinese) wife, Zhuping. My mom died shortly thereafter. Afterward, my sister, brother, and I went out to Gordon Biersch and threw back shots of whiskey. (It seemed when a parent died you drank whiskey. First time around anyway.) Like newly minted grown-ups, we began babbling to one another about our sex lives (why?).

We orchestrated the memorial for my mom on the back deck in my house in Van Nuys (where I would get married one year later). We moved our grand piano right out onto it. The memorial ended with the "Victory March" from *Aida*, waving palm fronds operatically to send my mother off into the cosmos. My sister would go on to scatter my mother's ashes all over the world—at the Paris Opera House, Egyptian pyramids, China's Great Wall.

Shortly thereafter, my mother came to me in an extremely vivid dream, so vivid it felt more real than life.

It was clear and extraordinary.

*Whoomp!*

*Fade into a panorama of mossy interconnecting small islands, like atolls. The air around us is heady, silvery. The sky is light.*

*Spirits whip by quickly. A soccer team in striped jerseys zips by on the left. Then the right. Then they zip into the horizon.*

*Just beyond, I see my mother joyously dipping in and out of the Pacific Ocean, like a dolphin. I run after her. It is a chase.*

*Because it is my reality and in this moment, if I wish it, I can make it so, I eventually do catch up with her. She sits down before me on a grassy berm. Her attitude toward me is gently loving and ever-so-slightly resigned to the fact that she has somehow agreed, in this space, to tarry a few minutes longer to humor a conversation, even though she would truly prefer to go on with her swimming and cavorting and joyousness, even though she knows I am going to be asking questions that make no difference, and to which her truthful responses will provide no satisfaction.*

*My first anguished questions: "When I came and visited you in the convalescent home, did you know I was there? Did you recognize me? Could you hear me?"*

*She looks at me carefully, as though weighing my anguish, and says kindly, but not very convincingly, "Yes. Oh yes. Of course."*

*I try some other questions to confirm various where, what, and whys, but the more trivial questions I try, the more a certain unknownness builds in the center.*

*A new idea comes to me, something I would never before have thought to ask: "So, can you tell me, what was your happiest day on earth?"*

*I anticipate that it will be the birth of my sister, or my brother's valedictorian speech, or perhaps my own graduation.*

*Her gray eyes looking out at the sea, my mother's dreamy answer is "Lunch with Betsy."*

*Betsy? There's no "Betsy" that I know of. But I immediately sense that "Betsy" was an amalgamation of that sort of very good neighbor/girlfriend/confidante, whom you could go to lunch with, or talk on the phone without censoring oneself, in that sort of floating hammock 3:15 pocket in the midafternoon. The free moment where you did not have to think about anyone else—their worries, fears, GPAs, groceries, or their other pressing CVS and Walgreen needs.*

*Then she says, "Oops, here come the sprinklers!"*

*Sprinklers erupt all around us on the green berm. She happily runs off and dives into the sea.*

*"No!" I yell, reaching out after her. But she is gone.*

THERE'S A KNOCK on the door. It's the funeral home.

The man who arrives is a large Caucasian man in an ever-so-slightly wrinkled black suit. It is disturbing. He is like one of those Town Car drivers who hold those signs up in baggage claim at LAX.

What was I hoping for? I suppose, like, two massage therapists from a Northern California luxury spa. Young beautiful UC Santa Cruz "wellness" majors in neutral hemp clothing. With lasers.

This dude looks a little Irish or a little Scottish, which is unusual for Los Angeles's Palmdale desert area, ruddy in complexion, with elaborately combed, lightly Brylcreemed hair, both full and thinning, in that LAX Town Car driver way. He has almost all of his teeth, but one toward the back that shouldn't be missing, is.

I almost wish instead our Styx crosser was a nice tidy Armenian gentleman, like the Lyft driver I recently had, in a shiny silver Camry with peppermint air freshener, and the exact perfect courteous sense to remind you what to do when you have forgotten.

This is for real and rather grim. It's as though my father is going to be clubbed over the head, blindfolded, driven to Ontario, and housed in an un-air-conditioned storage unit while thugs call uninterested family members unwilling to come up with the relatively small ransom. Like forty-five dollars. Like in a not-very-good reality show.

"Sorry for your loss," he says huskily, as though he himself has just come from knocking off a few people. Behind him, a bald dude in a tie wheels in a gurney, with straps. Both are wearing light blue surgical gloves.

"Have you said goodbye?" he asks with hooded eyes, waiting to do his job. And suddenly things get very real.

I realize this is the last time I will ever be in the same room as the physical form of my father, who is the same father I have known for fifty-six years. There are so many memories—beach swimming, fighting in airports, driving in cars as he ate expired sushi, college graduations, him falling asleep every Sunday afternoon in the sun in that circular wicker chair in our old Malibu house—

It all felt like it would never end— How many times had I sat at the Formica dining room table, in an earlier life, a life so remote it could well have happened to someone else—I saw the click of the clock on our yellow O'Keefe and Merritt stove. Time would proceed so slowly it actually appeared to move backward.

In five minutes the essence of him will be permanently lost. I am suddenly not ready.

We ask the Borg to leave and now I crouch next to my dad and begin to freak out. I anxiously stroke his now almost completely cool forehead and suddenly decide that I have to cut off and keep a lock of his gray-white straw-like hair. Thomas thinks that is a great idea, and that he should get some, too.

He immediately cannot find nail scissors. He has clippers? No. He finally finds some very tiny nail scissors. We each cut off a few hairs and fold them into a napkin. We suddenly giggle, madly, with a sense that we have gotten away with something.

We invite the undertaker back in and, cumbersomely, almost comically, he and his assistant utilize a sheet and pads and practically bungee cords to get my dad from the foam pad onto the gurney. It feels like with the fussy moving around and discreet curtaining of sheets and blankets they are actually making more work for themselves, and for us. ("One, two, three . . . hup.")

The gurney is wheeled out and the van doors close. That is it.

The undertaker's voice is oddly husky and high. Like one of the characters in a movie that then rips the mask off and underneath he is made of a column of weevils.

"Sorry about your loss. We'll take good care of him."

The coroner will take a few days to complete his official tasks, so my dad's body will lie in a refrigerated drawer for several days. But we don't know that then.

I go to Starbucks.

I take out all my dad's identification.

Here's his driver's license, from which he beams, in his big black glasses, his spirit eternally ready for another adventure. Five feet six inches and 122 pounds. So small? How is that possible? I cry.

My sister, brother, and I decide we will hold a memorial quickly, mostly for the sake of grieving Thomas and his family.

Unlike my mother with her big beautiful memorial, with the grand piano and opera music, my father's circle has shrunk. Almost none of his friends are still alive. The few who are are too frail to travel.

It's just going to be my friends and some of our old schoolmates from Malibu. Culling photos from old albums, it's astonishing to remember how vastly and vigorously my father traveled. There are photos of him at the Taj Mahal, cavorting with tribal villagers in Tanzania, belly dancing in Morocco, chasing penguins in Antarctica, and yes, in New Zealand . . . bungee jumping. At that particular sport site, over the age of sixty-five, bungee jumping was free, so he did it.

Throughout the world, ten years older than we are now, in between marriages, my father traveled alone but always found people with whom to eat, laugh, lift a glass. The younger—and blonder—and bustier, the better. In bathing suits, in beaches, under twinkling lights.

I point out to Charlie the continual preponderance, in photo after photo, of red plastic Solo "party" cups scattered across the scene. Big ones. I suggest that, along with champagne, we should offer margaritas in the red Solo cups that adorned so many of my father's ad hoc festive occasions.

The Malibu band Boy Hits Car—the stars of the *This American Life* piece about my father—reaches out. I ask whether they would agree to reprise their grunge rock song "Mr. Loh" on our back porch at sunset. In my mind these surf dudes are still twentysomethings, although my sister points out that Boy Hits Car must be, like us, approaching their sixties.

I am getting excited. My next idea is that as a backdrop we should string up Tibetan prayer flags interlaced with board shorts—the sorts of big colorful beach shorts that male body surfers wear. At the Third Eye Bookstore, I buy out their entire stock of Tibetan flags. This being Southern California, Goodwill has a ton of truly psychedelic board shorts, from two to four dollars each. I buy 97 pairs, for what I've decided I will call, in deference to my father's 97 years, "the traditional 97 board-short salute."

And I then decide that at the end of the song, as a rock 'n' roll tribute, we should all hold up lighters! I google local suppliers that create custom lighters. I scan a photo of my dad in a leopard Speedo. The guy sends me the proof. The picture is small, the resolution poor, the font is . . . ornate gold cursive? It looks gangsta. But appropriate?

*Mr. Loh*

*Not Afraid to Be Naked*

. . .

THE GUEST LIST IS, weirdly, ninety-seven strong. Everyone comes on time.

Andie, Julia, Marilyn.

Some Malibu school chums.

Zhuping, my dad's long-suffering second Chinese wife, with her new husband Steve. Charlie's Gentlemen Callers, in suit jackets.

And there are children, not just our cousin's son's Chi-Latino triplets, but so many other children.

Everyone has brought anything and everything chocolate, as asked.

We first sing "Danny Boy" together, in deference to so many who have died, whom we lost.

### DANNY BOY

*Oh, Danny Boy, the pipes, the pipes are calling*
*From glen to glen, and down the mountain side.*
*The summer's gone and all the roses falling,*
*It's you, it's you must go and I must bide.*
*But come ye back when summer's in the meadow,*
*Or when the valley's hushed and white with snow,*
*It's I'll be here in sunshine or in shadow,*
*Oh, Danny Boy, oh Danny Boy, I love you so!*
*But when ye come, and all the flowers are dying,*
*If I am dead, as dead I well may be,*
*You'll come and find the place where I am lying,*
*And kneel and say an Ave there for me.*
*And I shall hear, though soft you tread above me,*

*And all my grave will warmer, sweeter be,*
*For you will bend and tell me that you love me,*
*And I shall sleep in peace until you come to me!*

Then come the eulogies. My brother is up first. In an homage to our father, he begins by stripping—taking off his tie, shirt, and pants . . . getting down to a tiny black Speedo. Everyone screams. Although he is not our dad, my fifty-eight-year-old brother is in pretty good shape.

My brother gives a pretty tough and honest speech.

"My father was eccentric, which is something you learn to deal with as a child. He was also angry, what you might term today emotionally abusive. Yet here the three of us are today. We've had happy lives. How do you explain it? Well, my father would say most of the credit goes to our mom. So our legacy is not something we leave on our own—it's a combination of those around us."

Next up is Cousin Zhe, serious in his big trifocal glasses.

"Life was so hard in China, and then your dad insisted on visiting! He never asked, just came! My father spent two months' salary just entertaining your dad. It was terrible. We never recovered." Zhe sits down.

Now comes Tiger Aunt Kaitlin. As the five grandchildren look on, her speech somehow amazingly comes to . . .

"Here's the message to take from our father's life on this day. Don't fear anything! Embrace your life! Go travel! Try everything! You will never regret it!"

I am amazed. Tiger Aunt just did this whole "When they go low, we go high" Michelle Obama thing.

She has transformed the whole idea of my father into a stirring, inspirational, full- throated exhortation for us all to seize the world.

Sally raises her hand, speaks shyly. "The other day, I was walking home by my old preschool. I thought about grandpa dying. Which was a bit of a nonevent. He was just so old. But then I realized that just as preschool was over, now grandpa was over."

Her thirteen-year-old eyes widen, in wonder. "They were now in The Past."

Thomas presents an extensive video montage to show what my dad's daily life actually was like in the last few years. There is Thomas, feeding my dad, bathing him, clipping his toenails, dressing him up in snazzy costumes—fedora, blazer, red turtleneck, white tennis sweater, sporty Dodgers hoodie.

There are montages of Thomas carrying a kind of celebratory plaque of my father to the beach, weeping, getting on the RTD bus with it.

There is Thomas, standing at the Pacific, wind riffling through his hair, crying. I remembered a story that Thomas had actually held political office back in the Philippines, but got chased out in some sort of coup. He is very charismatic and soulful, his eyes full of tears, almost like a Bollywood star. Orchestral music swells.

The coup de grâce is when Thomas finally goes to the morgue and they pull my father out of the drawer. There is dramatic slow-motion video of Thomas flung over my father, weeping, like a pietà.

"Wow," Tex murmurs, "best memorial ever."


It's now sunset. We head to the deck. Ninety-seven board shorts and innumerable Tibetan prayer flags flutter. The children have found the Party Store bag of shitty Mardi Gras beads, and are flinging them into the trees. The cheap flimsy strands loop and twirl and sparkle.

"It's the Krewe of Mr. Loh," Bradford says wonderingly.
On guitars, Boy Hits Car croons their brooding homage against
the fading sun.

### "MR. LOH"

*by Boy Hits Car*

*As I can see the ocean breaking*
*The ocean breaks on herself*
*It will remind me that all the shit I'm feeling*
*Will soon be, will be alright, it's gonna be alright*

*Mr. Loh, he finds the water*
*And it seems to wash this place off*
*As the dolphins jump and play*

*He speaks to us in the sand*
*Do you know the meaning of life*
*Or are you just a simple man?*
*And then he swims away*
*Then he swims away*

*Mr. Loh, will you speak to me?*
*You're the only one I understand*
*Mr. Loh, will you sing to me?*
*You're the only one who makes sense*

*Mr. Loh's not afraid to be naked*
*But some men fall from grace*
*They're not secure with themselves*

*He doesn't measure people*
*By things we consider important*
*Can't seem to comprehend today*
*So he swims away, he swims away*
*Come back*

*Mr. Loh, will you speak to me?*
*You're the only one I understand*
*Mr. Loh, will you sing to me?*
*You're the only one who makes sense*

*Mr. Loh dialogue (done by my brother)*
*Contact with nature, now that's very important*
*All in society is so busy, busy, busy, busy*
*Not much time*
*Talk to yourself or talk to the nature*

*As long as I can see the ocean break on herself*
*As the dolphins jump and play*
*It will remind me, that all the shit I'm feeling*
*Will soon be alright*

*Mr. Loh, will you speak to me?*
*You're the only one I understand*
*Mr. Loh, will you sing to me?*
*You're the only one who makes sense*

*Oh Mr. Loh, oh Mr. Loh*
*This is gonna be alright*

Lighters go up. All of the children, ten and under, appear to have three lighters each.

The memorial is over.

We feast on Zankou Chicken. And chocolate, so much chocolate. For today, Mr. Loh's clan is all here.

Sam, who after his straight-A stint at community college, will get scholarship offers from UC Berkeley, UCLA, and on. After interviewing forty engineers, over Charlie's cries of "Berkeley! Berkeley! Berkeley!" Sam deduces that the best engineering school is Cal Poly San Luis Obispo.

He will proceed to become the unofficial den father of Mr. Loh's five one-quarter-Chinese grandchildren, making Google schedule alerts for Hannah and Wayne to complete for their college applications, every single one of which they miss. Tales for other days.

The Chi-Latino triplets are crowded into the massage chair. Hannah is tickling them.

Sabrina, "the Palace Cat," is sporting a small new tattoo on her ankle. It is the Dewey decimal system number for the fantasy section.

"Is that kid having . . . alcoholic punch?" Charlie asks, as a tot goes by with a red Solo cup.

"We get them started early," I say.

We laugh, hug each other, shake our shoulders out. Charlie is as much our family as any. Perhaps he, too, may be considered honorary part Chinese.

Two roads indeed diverged in a wood, many more fan out beyond.

One inadvertent protection for Mr. Loh's grandchildren: In California, Prop 13 keeps his Malibu property taxes superlow. At the expense of their public schools, but . . . If not a silver, at least a pewter, lining.

In the falling light, I see mementos of The Past, hunkering on the edges of the deck.

Sally's old red trike.

Our old Swiffer, of the Upstairs, Downstairs days. Hannah's blue IKEA student chair with the wobbly leg. The white tin "lice" bowl.

And I think for a moment, about the humble louse. The kinder, gentler pest. They don't sprout wings and fly around your head like bats. They're just quietly trying to get by. They don't have faces. They don't do much but itch.

On the one hand, the lice taught us science, because when we had them we soon learned the life cycle—eggs, nits, male and female, the physics of hair shafts.

But amid the frenzied hubbub of daily life, homework, projects, activities, lessons, the lice created some of our most beautiful time together. When else in childhood would I have taken hours and hours to comb through my daughters' hair? The boredom, the card games, joy of counting the dead bugs in the white tin.

Ah, well. For today, here are tipsy four-year-olds who got into the margarita punch, savoring their first Bic lighters.

Waving them, cackling, in the dark.

# Acknowledgments

THIS BOOK MARKS my twenty-fifth anniversary (a quarter century!) of writing publicly about my life. Over that time, I've moved exactly twenty miles, from Van Nuys to Pasadena, gone up a pants size or two (depending on stretch of material), married, divorced, moved from fake glasses into real ones. Friends have come and gone, and editors, theaters, and magazines. (I remember, in my early thirties, Clay Felker barking over the phone, "Sandra! What's hot in Los Angeles?," and literally having no clue: that one was for *M Inc.*) Things writers used to complain about are now the past's gold standard. Monthly *Buzz* magazine lunches at Maple Drive—Maple Drive!—had tricky parking. Oh how we'd complain, over $1.50 coffees, about the editors at our alternative weeklies. There *were* alternative weeklies. The late Jonathan Gold was my first (music) editor. I knew the late Andrew before there was a Breitbart.

So, in a perhaps quasi-Asian way, as I acknowledge a ghost world, I also thank folks and institutions that are still present. KCRW and then KPCC gave my weekly radio series, *The Loh Life*, twenty years, which grew the heart of this book's material. *This American Life* also resonates here (my father!): I thank Ira Glass. I wish I'd written a bit faster for David Wallace-Wells. I can't believe that Adam Shulman (Left Coast—twenty-five years) and Sloan Harris (Right Coast— thirty years) are still my agents, or whatever important packaging managing partner thing they are now. I'm so lucky today to write for Jill Bialosky.

Now to the tricky part (as though that Breitbart reference wasn't tricky enough—but he was funny and wore rubber pool sandals to my late friend Cathy Seipp's parties, that's all I knew then, I swear!). Acknowledgments can be where you messily try to sort your "thanks" out. But it's impossible to do it right. You want to note a witty thing someone said, but that person asks you not to mention their signature Top-Siders, so you change that detail, putting them in Crocs, without remembering that someone else wore Crocs, and the original speaker (who has since changed his/her/their mind) would never wear Crocs, and now both people are furious (via a rapidly-unspooling group text message with many emoticons). Even when you try to ensure that you always come off the worst (because that is truth), you don't always succeed.

So there are many people whose hilarity and humanity I would like to acknowledge but who, for various reasons, I can't. I honor them, at home, in private, before my Dr. Loh shrine (another long story). I can say that I have some very amusing Facebook friends (who care about both their real and fake teeth). There is, always, my lovely Peggy, with both her moral integrity *and* her Native American jewelry. As great soundboards in my ongoing puzzling over "Asian-American-ness," I thank wise and witty Kip Fulbeck and Alice Tuan. My life has been brightened by my two (two!) age-appropriate Pokémon Go friends, Athenaskana and TheHedonist—we've traded Pokémon gifts while I visited the Huntington Gardens to, er, "write" (my Pokémon name is AngryOldLady). A salute to Anna Hubler, Richard Roat,

Wendy Mogel. Model couples: Maggie and Barry, Irene and Ken, Beverly and Marc (who has a beautiful colon). I'm lucky to know some hella smart and amusing women: Caroline Aaron, Anny Celsi, Danette Christine, Samantha Dunn, Murielle Hamilton, Shannon Holt, Gina Kronstadt, Irene Lacher, Susan Marder, Deb Vogel. Ink-stained wretches Erika Schickel, and I cry and write in the Dena's, where, sadly, today the coffee is much more than $1.50. Hilarious dudes, and they know why: Dan Akst, Bart Delorenzo, the Rogers, Neill and Trilling, Carlos (Car-los!) Rodriguez, Max Schwartz, Dave Shulman, David Schweizer and our deep philosophical carb conversations, which should become their own modern opera, and Jim Turner (we will always have the produce aisle at the Glendale Costco, but the massage chair is *mine*).

I thank Frier McCollister, a true flaneur and boulevardier of the old school.

I thank Madeline Peng Miller and Tsing Miller for their brilliance and heart.

I thank Jacobsen Paul Loh, a stellar guy.

And—check out this turn—I never would have have anticipated this—I thank Malibu. Not just the Malibu West Beach Club and the grunge band Boy Hits Car (thanks, Cregg Rondell!), who gave my strange Chinese father such a happy home. I mean what we call Old Malibu—I still have some great f@#$ing friends . . . from middle and high school! Jennifer Field, Karen Foster, Jim Lorick, Susan Sachs! Even as adolescents, boarding the school bus (the ride took hours), enduring bizarre counselors, running timed miles (did we?), there was always the lifted eyebrow above the viola case, as a skateboarder slammed into one: "You are not alone."

And that's where we end: kindness in childhood. An earlier memoir, *Mother on Fire*, charted my worry at my first child's starting kindergarten in public school in Los Angeles—and by that I mean "the hood," Van Nuys. Fifteen years later, as my kids enter college, I honor their truly wonderful Valley schools, full of so much joy, curiosity, and rigor: Valley Alternative Magnet (and Ellen Rubin), Carlos Lauchu's "Ventura Hogwarts," and Van Nuys High (Randy Olea). And of course, Yamillah, one of life's unsung heroines, who, even at age six, was good people. Never change.